The Ret
OF THE
Lord Jesus

BY

DR. R. A. TORREY D.D.

The Return of the Lord Jesus

This edition 1997

ISBN 1 898787 91 3

AMBASSADOR PRODUCTIONS LTD,
Providence House
16 Hillview Avenue,
Belfast, BT5 6JR
Northern Ireland

Emerald House,
1 Chick Springs Road, Suite 206
Greenville,
South Carolina 29609
United States of America

Synopsis

PRELIMINARY STATEMENTS

CHAPTER I.

THE IMPORTANCE OF THE TRUTH THAT OUR LORD JESUS IS COMING AGAIN.

CHAPTER II.

THE CERTAINTY THAT OUR LORD JESUS IS COMING AGAIN.

CHAPTER III.

THE MANNER IN WHICH OUR LORD JESUS IS COMING AGAIN.

Preliminary Statements

The writer an optimist—His optimism defined The true doctrine of the advent is: A safeguard against error — The most precious truth.

"This word He hath in fact spoken,—'Hereafter ye shall see the Son of Man coming in the clouds of heaven,'—but it is a word of which there is no example. Even the mad pride of Roman emperors who demanded religious homage for their statutes has never gone so far as to conceive such an unheard of thought, and here it is the lowliest of men who speaks.. The word must be truth; for there is here no mean term between truth and madness."

LUTHARDT.

Preliminary Statements

THE writer of this book is an optimist. He is absolutely sure that a golden age is swiftly coming to this earth. But he is not a blind optimist. His optimism is not the result of shutting his eyes to unpleasant facts; his eyes are wide open to the awful injustices that rule in human society as at present constituted. He is fully aware that there is a storm coming. He does not question that we are facing the wildest, fiercest, most appalling storm this old world ever passed through, but the storm will be brief and beyond the storm there is a golden day, such as philosophers and poets never dreamed of. The writer is an optimist because he has deeply pondered and believes with his whole heart what the Bible teaches concerning the Second Coming of Christ. If he did not believe that, he could not but be a pessimist, knowing what he does of social conditions and the trend of human society today. In the Return of our Lord is the perfect solution, and the only solution, of the political and social and commercial problems that now vex us.

In the truth concerning our Lord's Return is the safeguard against all current heresies, errors and falsehoods. One error after another is arising to deceive, if it were possible, even the very elect. One who knows the truth clearly revealed in God's Word concerning the Second Coming of Christ is proof against them all. For example, no one who knows the truth concerning the Second Coming of Christ could possibly be misled by Christian Science, Millenial Dawnism, Occultism, Theosophy or Behaism. It is remarkable how all forms of error touch the doctrine of Christ's Second Coming, and are shattered by the truth revealed about it in the Scriptures. Those who are ignorant of what the Word teaches concerning the Second Coming of Christ may fancy that they see in Madame Besant's "Order of the Star of the East" a preparation for the coming of Christ, but those who know the truth know that it is a preparation for the welcoming of the Antichrist, the Devil's imitation Christ.

The truth of our Lord's Return is the most precious truth the Bible contains. It fills the heart of the believer with joy, and girds him with strength for the battle. It lifts him above the sorrows and fears and necessities and trials and ambitions and greed of this world and makes him in all things more than conqueror.

All the quotations in this book are taken from the American Standard Version of the Bible. There can be little doubt that on the whole this version comes nearer to giving the exact and full force of the original than any other version now in common use, and space is saved by quoting directly from it in every case instead of quoting the Authorized Version and then putting in the margin the Revised Version, or the American Standard Version.

Chapter I.

THE IMPORTANCE OF THE TRUTH THAT OUR LORD JESUS IS COMING AGAIN.

The frequency of its mention—Its emphasis as the comfort of saints and the blessed hope of the believer—It is peculiarly obnoxious to the worldly—It is the incentive to service, watchfulness and separation—Four stages of the author's experience — The transformation wrought in him by the apprehension of the doctrine.

"Ye turned from the idols to serve a living and true God, and to wait for His Son from Heaven, whom He raised from the dead, even Jesus, who delivereth us from the wrath to come."

I THESSALONIANS 1:9, 10.

"For what is our hope, or joy, or crown of rejoicing? Are not even ye, before our Lord Jesus Christ at His coming."

1 THESSALONIANS 2:19.

"Amen: come, Lord Jesus."

REVELATION 22:20.

CHAPTER I

THE IMPORTANCE OF THE TRUTH THAT OUR LORD JESUS IS COMING AGAIN

THE importance in God's thought of the Second Coming of Christ is seen in the fact that this event is mentioned more times in the New Testament than there are chapters. It has been said by those who have taken the trouble to count that it is mentioned 318 times in the 260 chapters of the New Testament. And one who made a life-long study of the doctrine has said that it occupies one in every twenty-five verses from Matthew to Revelation. It also occupies a prominent place in the Old Testament, as by far the greater part of the predictions concerning Christ in the Old Testament are connected, not with His first coming to die as an atoning Saviour, but with His Second Coming to rule as King.

The coming again of Jesus Christ is the one

doctrine with which God commands us to comfort sorrowing saints. When death had begun to thin the ranks of the believers in Thessalonica, and hearts were aching over separation from those who had fallen asleep, the Apostle Paul wrote, "But we would not have you ignorant, brethren, concerning them that fall asleep; that ye sorrow not, even as the rest who have no hope. For if we believe that Jesus died and rose again, even so them also that are fallen asleep in Jesus will God bring with him. For this we say unto you by the word of the Lord, that we that are alive, that are left unto the coming of the Lord, shall in no wise precede them that are fallen asleep. For the Lord Himself shall descend from heaven, with a shout, with the voice of the archangel, and with the trump of God; and the dead in Christ shall rise first; then we that are alive, that are left, shall together with them be caught up in the clouds, to meet the Lord in the air; and so shall we ever be with the Lord. Wherefore, *comfort one another with these words*" (I Thess. 4:13-18). As "these words" have entirely to do with the Second Coming of Christ, it is evident that the one doctrine with which God commands us to comfort those in sorrow over the loss of loved ones is that of our Lord's Coming again. There is no other truth that has such comfort in it for intelligent believers when they are called upon to pass through deep sorrow as that of the Return of the Lord and what it involves for us and for those who have fallen asleep. Time and again in writing to those who have lost for a time those whom they love, I have obeyed God's commandment and used the truth of our Lord's Return to comfort them, and many have told me afterwards how full of comfort this truth has proven when everything else had failed. In the Old Testament also we find God through His servant Isaiah comforting Israel in the time of their misery and desolation with the thought of the Coming of the Lord: "Comfort ye, comfort ye my people, saith your God. O thou that tellest good tidings to Zion, get thee up on a high mountain; O thou that tellest good tidings to Jerusalem, lift up thy voice with strength; lift it up, be not afraid; say unto the cities of Judah, Behold, your God! Behold, his reward is with him and his recompense before him" (Is. 40:1, 9, 10).

Time and again in the New Testament the Coming Again of our Lord Jesus Christ and the events connected therewith are held up as "the blessed hope" and the eager desire of every true believer. In Titus 2:13 Paul says, "Looking for the blessed hope and appearing of the glory of the great God and our Saviour Jesus Christ." And Peter in II Peter 3:11, says: "Seeing that these things are thus all to be dissolved, what manner of persons ought ye to be in all holy living and godliness, *looking for and earnestly desiring* the coming of the day of God, by reason of which the heavens being on fire shall be dissolved, and the elements shall melt with fervent heat?" To the true believer, the Coming Again of Jesus Christ is not something to dread, but it is the brightest hope the future holds for us and it should be the object of our eager desire and longing anticipation. The last prayer in the Bible is also the cry of every intelligent Christian heart, "Amen; come, Lord Jesus" (Rev. 22:20).

But while the Return of our Lord is the blessed hope and eager desire of the true believer, it is the particular object of the hatred and ridicule of the mockers who walk after their own lusts. Peter's prediction has come true: "In the last days mockers shall come with mockery, walking after their own lusts, and saying, Where is the promise of His coming? for, from the day that the fathers fell asleep, all things continue as they were from the beginning of the creation'' (II Pet. 3:3, 4). A worldly Church and worldly Christians join with these mockers in their hatred of this truth. As a bride who is flirting with other men does not long for the return of her absent husband, so the faithless bride of Christ, who is flirting with the world does not long for the return of her Lord. But for the believer whose affections are all fixed upon Jesus Christ the Word of God contains no other promise so precious as the promise that He is quickly coming again. Our attitude toward the Coming Again of Jesus Christ is a good index of our spiritual state.

The fact that our Lord Jesus is coming again is the great Bible argument for a life of watchfulness, fidelity, wisdom, activity, simplicity, self-restraint, prayer and abiding in Christ. During the last week of His earthly life, our Lord said to His disciples, ''Therefore be ye also ready; *for in an hour that ye think not the son of man cometh''* (Matt. 24:44). In our day we are constantly urging men to be ready because death may overtake them at any moment, but this was not the argument that our Lord Jesus used. It was

His own coming, not the coming of death, that He held up before His disciples as the incentive to live as they ought to live. Proceeding still further, He said, "Who then is the faithful and wise servant, whom his lord hath set over his household, to give them food in due season? Blessed is that servant whom *his lord when he cometh* shall find so doing" (vs. 45.46). On another occasion our Lord was warning His disciples against the sins which are especially common in our day, over-eating, over-drinking, and undue occupation with the cares of this life, "Take heed to yourselves," He said, "lest haply your hearts be overcharged with surfeiting and drunkenness, and cares of this life, *and that day come on you suddenly as a snare*: for so shall it come upon all that dwell on the face of all the earth. But watch ye at every season making supplication, that ye may prevail to escape all these things that shall come to pass, and to stand before the Son of Man" (Luke 21:34-36). It was not the physical effects of folly in eating and drinking that our Lord urged upon His disciples but rather the fact that these things would unfit them to meet Him upon His Return. The Apostle John writes to those whom he had led into the light, "Now, little children, abide in Him; that, if He shall be manifested, we may have boldness, and not be *ashamed before Him at His coming*" (I John 2:28). There are many reasons why we should abide in the Lord Jesus but the pre-eminent reason in John's mind was that Jesus was coming again and that if we were to have confidence and not be ashamed before Him when He did come, we must be abiding in Him.

Our Lord Jesus tells us that His return is the one event for which we should be looking. "Let your loins be girded about," He says, "and your lamps burning; and be ye yourselves like unto men *looking for their lord* when he shall return from the marriage feast; that, when he cometh and knocketh, they may straightway open unto him." (Luke 12:35, 36). In the next verse an especial blessing is pronounced upon those "*Whom the Lord when He cometh shall find watching.*" The Holy Spirit in the 9th chapter of Hebrews and the 28th verse tells us that "*to them that wait for Him,*" shall He "appear a second time apart from sin unto salvation." These words ought to lead us to some very deep and earnest thinking and to ask ourselves whether we are really looking, watching, waiting for Him.

It is evident from what has been said above, that the truth of our Lord's Second Coming is a truth of the very first importance. To many the doctrine of the Second Coming of Christ seems like an impractical doctrine. I once so regarded it. In my early ministry, one of my members came to me and asked if I would speak upon the Second Coming of Christ. I knew nothing about the doctrine and put him off, thinking to myself, "You will be a much older man than you are now before I speak upon a doctrine so impractical." But the day came when I found it was not only one of the most precious but also one of the most practical doctrines in the whole Bible. There have been four marked epochs in my Christian experience: First, When I came to know the Lord Jesus as my personal Saviour and my Lord. Second, When I discovered that the Bible was indeed the inerrant Word of God, that its statements were absolutely reliable in every respect, and that everything any man needed to know was contained in this one Book. Third, When I learned that the baptism with the Holy Spirit was for the present day and claimed it for myself. And Fourth,

When I came to see the truth concerning the Second Coming of Christ. The latter truth transformed my whole idea of life, it broke the power of the world and its ambition over me and filled my life with the most radiant optimism even under the most discouraging circumstances.

Chapter II.

THE CERTAINTY THAT OUR LORD JESUS IS COMING AGAIN.

It is repeatedly and explicitly affirmed by the Word of God—It is distinguished as a coming "a second time"—It is not synonymous with death—It is not the coming of the Holy Spirit—It did not occur at the destruction of Jerusalem—It lies yet in the future.

"He who testifieth these things saith, yea: (surely) I come quickly. Amen: come Lord Jesus."

REVELATION 22:20.

CHAPTER II

THE CERTAINTY THAT OUR LORD JESUS IS COMING AGAIN

BEYOND a peradventure our Lord Jesus is coming again. How do we know that? Because God tells us so in His Word, over and over again in the most explicit and unmistakable terms. On the night before His crucifixion our Lord Jesus seeking to comfort His disciples who were overwhelmed with the thought that He was about to leave them said, "*I come again* and will receive you unto myself; that where I am, there ye may be also" (John 14:3). The Apostle Paul in I Thess. 4:16, 17 takes up this promise of his Lord and writes, "*The Lord Himself shall descend* from heaven, with a shout, with the voice of the archangel, and with the trump of God; and the dead in Christ shall rise first; then we that are alive that are left, shall together with them be caught up in the clouds, to meet the Lord in the air: and so shall we ever be with the Lord." The Apostle Paul doubtless had the words of Christ in mind when he said this; for there are four items in connection with the Lord's promise that are exactly covered by four in Paul's words. (1) Jesus said, "I come again." Paul said, "The Lord Himself shall descend from heaven." (2) Jesus said, "and receive you unto myself." Paul said, "We shall be caught up to meet the Lord." (3) Jesus said, "that where I am there ye may be also." Paul said, "So shall we ever be with the Lord." (4) Jesus prefaces His words with "Let not your heart be troubled" (John 14:1). Paul closes his by saying, "Comfort one another with these words." Paul's words are an inspired commentary upon the promise of Jesus.

In one of his later epistles Paul says again, "Our citizenship is in heaven; *whence also we wait for a Saviour,* the Lord Jesus Christ: who shall fashion anew the body of our humiliation, that it may be conformed to the body of His glory, according to the working whereby he is able even to subject all things unto himself" (Phil. 3:20, 21). In Heb. 9:28 we read again, "Christ also, having been once offered to bear the sins of many, shall *appear a second time* apart from sin, to them that wait for him, unto salvation.'' The Apostle Peter in urging the Jews to repentance in Acts 3:19-21 says, ''Repent ye, therefore, and turn again, that your sins may be blotted out, that so there may come seasons of refreshing from the presence of the Lord; and *that he may send the Christ* who hath been appointed for you, even Jesus: whom the heaven must receive until the times of restoration of all things, whereof God spake by the mouth of his holy prophets that have been from of old.'' All the passages quoted, as well as many others, assert in the most distinct and unambiguous terms that OUR LORD JESUS IS COMING AGAIN.

There are those who would interpret at least some of these passages as referring to the death of the believer, but the passages will not admit of this interpretation. At the death of the believer, while our Lord Jesus may draw near, He does not come ''with a shout,'' nor ''with the voice of the archangel,'' nor ''with the trump of God.'' At the death of the believer, those who are alive and left surely are not caught up with them to meet the Lord in the air. Jesus Himself drew a plain contrast between the death of the believer and His own coming again. Speaking to Peter about the future of John He said, "If I will that he (John) tarry till I come, what is that to thee?" It is plain from the context that "If I will that he tarry" means, "If I will that he remain alive." Now if we put Christ's coming at the believer's death, then we would get this nonsense, "If I will that he remain alive until he die, what is that to thee?" Of course, it is not what our Lord meant. What He meant, as is plainly indicated by the words in their context, was "If I will that he remain alive until my own personal return."

There are others who would have us interpret the coming again spoken of in the verses above as referring to the coming of Christ at the coming of the Holy Spirit. The coming of the Holy Spirit is doubtless in a very real and important sense a coming of Christ. This appears from John 14:15-18; 20-23, where Jesus says, "If ye love me ye will keep my commandments. And I will pray the Father, and he shall give you another Comforter, that he may be with you forever; even the Spirit of truth; whom the world cannot receive, for it beholdeth him not, neither knoweth him: ye know him; for he abideth with you, and shall be in you. I will not leave you desolate: I come unto you. . . . He that hath my commandments, and keepeth them, he it is that loveth me: and he that loveth me shall be loved of my Father, and I will love him, and will manifest myself unto him. Judas (not Iscariot) saith unto him, Lord, what is come to pass that thou wilt manifest thyself unto us, and not unto the world? Jesus answered and said unto him, If a man love me, he will keep my word: and my Father will love him, and *we will come unto him,* and make our abode with him." It is plain from these words that the coming of the Holy Spirit is a coming of Jesus Christ, because it is His work to reveal Christ to us and to form Christ in us, so that Christ comes to make His abode with us; but this coming of Christ is not that which is referred to in the passages under consideration. This is evident from the fact that all these promises but one (John 14:3) were made after the coming of the Holy Spirit and pointed to a coming still future. Furthermore, Jesus at the coming of the Holy Spirit does not receive us unto Himself to be with Him, rather He comes to be with us (John 14:18, 21, 23), but at His coming again mentioned in John 14:3, and I Thess. 4:16, 17, He takes us to be with Him. Further still, He does not at His coming in the Spirit fashion anew the body of our humiliation that it may be conformed to the body of His glory (Phil. 3:20, 21), and at the coming of the Spirit, there is no trump of the archangel, no shout, no resurrection, no rapture in the clouds—in other words the coming of Christ at the coming of the Holy Spirit in scarcely any particular conforms to the plain and explicit statements of Christ and the Apostles concerning His Second Coming.

Many scholarly students of the Bible, whose opinion is well worth considering, take the coming again mentioned in the verses above to be at the Destruction of Jerusalem. There is an element of truth in this interpretation. The destruction of Jerusalem was in an important sense a precursor, prophecy and type of the judgment of the end of this age and therefore in Matt. 24 and Mark 13 the two events are described in connection with each other. But God's judgment on Jerusalem at that time is manifestly not the event referred to in the passages given in the opening of this chapter. At the destruction of Jerusalem, those who slept in Jesus were not raised, living believers were not caught up to meet the Lord in the air, the bodies of believers were not transformed. Furthermore, years after the destruction of Jerusalem we find John still looking forward to the Lord's coming as an event still lying in the future (Rev. 22:20). The words found in John 21:22, 23, "Jesus saith unto him, If I will that he tarry till I come, what is that to thee? Follow thou me. This saying therefore went forth among the brethren, that that disciple should not die: yet Jesus said not unto him, He should not die; but, If I will that he tarry till I come, what is that to thee?" were written years after the destruction of Jerusalem.

Not any of these events mentioned, nor all of them together, nor any other event that has yet occurred fulfills the very plain, explicit and definite predictions and promises of our Lord Jesus and His apostles regarding His coming again. THE COMING AGAIN OF JESUS CHRIST SO FREQUENTLY MENTIONED IN THE NEW TESTAMENT AS THE GREAT HOPE OF THE CHURCH IS AN EVENT THAT STILL LIES IN THE FUTURE.

Chapter III.

THE MANNER IN WHICH OUR LORD JESUS IS COMING AGAIN.

Personally—Bodily and visibly—In three stages —With great publicity—In great power and glory—With His holy angels—Suddenly and unannounced.

"And while they were looking steadfastly into heaven as he went, behold, two men stood by them in white apparel; who also said, Ye men of Galilee, why stand ye looking into heaven? this Jesus, who was received up from you into heaven, shall so come in like manner as ye behold Him going into heaven."

ACTS 1:10, 11.

CHAPTER III

THE MANNER IN WHICH OUR LORD JESUS IS COMING AGAIN

THAT our Lord Jesus is coming again is generally admitted among all who really believe in the Bible, but there is a wide diversity of opinion as to how He is coming again. However, if one will go to the Bible to find out what it teaches, instead of trying to read his own views into the Bible, there are many things about the Manner of His Coming which are perfectly plain.

I. First of all, it is perfectly plain that *His coming will be personal.* That is to say, it is not merely the coming of some great revival, or moral reformation, or social uplift, or the disclosure of some new truth, but the coming of our Lord Jesus Himself. In His promise to His disciples on the night of His crucifixion, He said, "*I* will come again." And the context clearly shows that He meant that

He personally was coming. The apostle Paul wrote, "*The Lord Himself shall descend from heaven.*" And the two men who stood by the disciples as they were looking steadfastly into heaven, trying to follow Jesus with their eyes as He went away from them, said, "Ye men of Galilee, why stand ye looking into heaven? *this Jesus* who was received up from you into heaven, shall so come in like manner as ye beheld Him going into heaven" (Acts 1:11). There is no mistaking the meaning of these words. *Jesus Himself in His own person* (the same Jesus who went away) is coming back again. Some years ago a minister of the Gospel wrote, "We must not expect a personal return of our Lord, but be satisfied with Him as coming more and more in all the wonders and glories of this closing nineteenth century." The man who wrote these words was a good and godly man, a man who had made great sacrifices for the Lord Jesus Christ, but I have never been able to comprehend how any man who really loved the Lord could have written these words. The wonders and glories of the closing nineteenth century were well enough in their place, and for them we thank God, but if one really loves the Lord, it is not the wonders and glories that He works that we long for, but for Jesus Himself. As much as we rejoice in His works, *it is Himself* that we long for; it is *Himself* that we must have; and it is *Himself* that we shall have. Suppose a bridegroom had left his bride and gone into a distant land to prepare a home for her, assuring her that in due time he would himself return for her to take her to the home that he had gone to prepare. Every now and then he has sent her some gift as a remembrance and a token of his continued love. One day a friend calls upon the bride and finds her eagerly looking forward to the day when the bridegroom himself shall return for her. After listening to her declaration of her longing for the return of the loved one, he says to her, "You must not expect a personal return of your husband. When he told you he would come again, he did not refer to a personal return. Has he not sent you many gifts as tokens of his love?" "Yes." "Well it is not for himself that you must look—you must learn to see him and be satisfied with him as coming to you more and more in the gifts which he is sending you from time to time." What would the bride reply? She would answer, "I do not desire his gifts. I am longing for himself." And it is for JESUS HIMSELF that the true believer is longing. We cannot be satisfied with him as coming more and more in the richer experiences of grace that are constantly coming to us by the power of the Holy Spirit. We long for Himself and we must have Himself and we shall have Himself. "This very Jesus, which was taken up into heaven shall so come in like manner" as He was seen to go into heaven.

II. The verses already quoted make clear a second thing about the coming again of our Lord, that is, *He shall come* BODILY AND VISIBLY. He "shall so come *in like manner as*" He was seen going into heaven (Acts 1:11). By any fair interpretation this can mean nothing short of a visible and bodily coming. It may mean more than that. It cannot mean less. It has been said that the expression "so come in like manner" only indicates the certainty of His coming, and has nothing to do with the manner of His Coming, but the Greek words thus translated will not admit of this construction. The literal translation of the Greek words is "Thus shall come in the manner which," and the form of expression is never used anywhere to indicate mere certainty, but always to indicate manner. *In the very manner* in which they had seen Him go would He come again. He had gone from their sight bodily and visibly. They had "*beheld* Him going into heaven" and should behold Him coming again. Furthermore, in Heb. 9:28 we read, "So Christ also, having been once offered to bear the sins of many, shall *appear* a second time, apart from sin, to them that wait for Him, unto salvation." The Greek word translated "shall appear" means literally "*shall be seen.*" The word admits of no significance but that of seeing with the eye. If possible, it is even clearer in Rev. 1:7, "Behold, he cometh with the clouds; *and every eye shall see him.*" Once at the close of a sermon on the Second Coming of Christ, a devoted disciple of Pastor Russell and his Millenial Dawn vagaries approached me and said, "You do not think, do you, that Jesus when He comes again will actually be seen with the eye?" I replied, "It does not matter what I think, the only question is, what does God's Word say? and God says in so many words in His Word, "Behold He cometh with the clouds; *and every eye shall see Him.*" Of course this does not fit in with the teaching of the Millenial Dawn books, that He has already come, nor does it fit in with many other current theories, but it is the plain teaching of the Word of God and cannot be escaped, except by such a juggling with God's Word as if applied to other passages of the Word would lead to utter confusion. If the Bible teaches anything definitely and distinctly, it teaches that the Lord Jesus who was taken up visibly and bodily from Mt. Olivet into heaven, so that the disciples saw Him as He went, is coming again visibly and bodily, so that people shall *see* Him as he comes. We shall not merely feel His spiritual presence near; we shall *see* Him, as really and as distinctly as the disciples saw Him as He stood talking with them on Mt. Olivet the moment before His feet left this earth and He was received up unto the Father.

There are to be different stages of this personal, visible coming of our Lord.

1. The first stage in His coming will be as He comes in the air whither His believing people shall be caught up to meet Him. "The Lord Himself shall descend from heaven with a shout, with the voice of the archangel, and with the trump of God; and the dead in Christ shall rise first; then we that are alive, that are left, *shall together with them be caught up in the clouds to meet the Lord in the air*: and so

shall we ever be with the Lord" (I Thess. 4:16, 17, R. V).

2. A second stage will be when He comes to the earth. "The Son of Man shall come in His glory, and all the angels with Him, then shall he sit on the throne of his glory; and before him shall be gathered all the nations; and he shall separate them one from the other, as the shepherd separateth the sheep from the goats" (Matt. 25:31, 32). "And his feet shall stand in that day upon the mount of Olives, which is before Jerusalem on the east; and the mount of Olives shall be cleft in the midst thereof toward the east and toward the west, and there shall be a very great valley; and half of the mountain shall remove toward the north, and half of it toward the south. And ye shall flee by the valley of my mountains; for the valley of the mountains shall reach unto Azel; yea, ye shall flee, like as ye fled from before the earthquake in the days of Uzziah King of Judah; and Jehovah my God shall come, and all the holy ones with thee" (Zech. 14:4, 5). From the closing words of the preceding quotation, it is evident that in this latter stage, His saints shall come with Him. This is also evident from I Thess. 3:13, "To the end he may establish

your hearts unblamable in holiness before our God and Father, at the coming of our Lord Jesus *with all His saints,*" and I Thess. 4:14, "For if we believe that Jesus died and rose again, even so them also that are fallen asleep in Jesus will God bring *with Him.*" In the air our Lord comes for His own; to the earth He comes with His own. For anything we know a considerable interval may take place between these two stages of the Lord's coming. The words of our Lord Himself in Luke 21:36 "But watch ye at every season making supplication, that ye may prevail *to escape all these things* that shall come to pass, and to stand before the Son of Man," and the words of Paul in II Thess. 2:7, 8, "For the mystery of lawlessness doth already work; only there is one that restraineth now, *until he be taken out of the way.* And *then* shall be revealed the lawless one, whom the Lord Jesus shall slay with the breath of his mouth, and bring to naught by the manifestation of his coming," seem to hint that the whole period of the great tribulation intervenes between the coming of Jesus in the air for His earthly saints and His coming to the earth with His saints. This, however, does not constitute two comings but two stages in the one coming. Bearing in mind the distinction between these two stages in His Coming Again will help to solve many of the seeming discrepancies between different texts of the Bible on this subject.

3. A third stage is a succession of events that follow His coming to the earth. Of these we shall speak more at length when we come to study results of His coming.

III. OUR LORD JESUS IS COMING AGAIN WITH GREAT PUBLICITY.

Our Lord Himself laid great emphasis upon this fact and warned His disciples against all those false prophets and teachers who should proclaim a secret coming. He said, "Then if any man shall say unto you, Lo, here is the Christ, or, Here; believe it not. For there shall arise false Christs, and false prophets, and shall show great signs and wonders; so as to lead astray, if possible, even the elect. Behold, I have told you beforehand. If therefore they shall say unto you, Behold, he is in the wilderness; go not forth. Behold, he is in the inner chambers; believe it not. *For as the lightning cometh forth from the east, and is seen even unto the west; so* shall be the coming of the Son of Man" (Matt. 24:23-27). We are being constantly told in these days that Jesus has come again in one person or in another, or in some new form of faith. One false teacher assures us that the second advent of the Lord Jesus Christ took place in October, 1874. Another school of error would have us believe that the revelation of the doctrines of Christian Science to Mary Baker Eddy was the Second Coming of Christ. Others have gone to the heart of Persia to find Him. Claims of a similar character are being constantly made in various quarters and a large society is now being formed in different parts of the world to watch for "the star in the east." These "inner chamber" Christs and obscure corner Christs are a humbug, long since predicted and exploded. If Christian people were more intelligent and careful students of the Word along these lines, they would not so readily fall a prey to these false teachings regarding Him. Our Lord was so careful to put us on our guard. Even at His coming for His saints there seems to be a large measure of publicity about it. We are told, "The Lord Himself shall descend from heaven, *with a shout,* with the voice of the archangel, and the *trump of God;* and the dead in Christ shall rise first." The doctrine of the secret rapture of believers does not seem to have much support in Scripture.

IV. When our Lord comes again, *He is coming on the clouds of heaven with POWER AND GREAT GLORY.* His words regarding it were, "And then shall appear the sign of the Son of man in heaven: and then shall all the tribes of the earth mourn, and they shall see the Son of man coming *on the clouds of heaven with power and great glory*" (Matt. 24:30, R. V). What did our Lord mean by saying He was coming on the clouds? First of all, this is a literal description of the manner of His coming, but further than that, it sets forth the fact that He is coming as a Divine person and in Divine glory. Everywhere in the Old Testament Jehovah was the One who came in or on a cloud. In Ex. 19:9, R. V., we read, "And *Jehovah* said unto Moses, Lo, *I come unto thee in a thick cloud,* that the people may hear when I speak with thee, and may also believe thee forever." Again we read in Ex. 34:5, "And *Jehovah* descended *in the cloud,* and stood with him there, and proclaimed the name of Jehovah." In Ps. 97:1, 2, the Psalmist sings, "*Jehovah* reigneth; let the earth rejoice; Let the multitudes of isles be glad. *Clouds and darkness are round about him*: Righteousness and justice are the foundation of his throne." Turning to the New Testament we read, "While he was yet speaking, *behold, a bright cloud* overshadowed them; and behold, a voice out of the cloud, saying, This is my beloved Son, in whom I am well pleased; hear ye him" (Matt. 17:5). In Ps. 104:3 it is written, "Who layeth the beams of his chambers in the waters; who *maketh the clouds HIS chariot;* Who walketh upon the wings of the wind." And in Is. 19:1, "Behold, *Jehovah rideth upon a swift cloud.*" From all these passages, it is plain that it is Jehovah who comes in the clouds or on a cloud, therefore to say that Jesus is coming in the clouds is to say that He is coming as a Divine person in Divine glory.

V. When our Lord Jesus comes again, *He is coming in the glory of His Father with the holy angels.* He Himself said so. In one place, Matt. 16:27, He says, "For the Son of man shall come *in the glory of his Father with his angels;* and then shall he render unto every man according to his deeds." And in Mark 8:38, He says, "For whosoever shall be ashamed of me and of my words in this adulterous and sinful generation, the Son of man also shall be ashamed of him when he cometh *in the glory of his Father with the holy angels.*" In a similar strain in II Thess. 1:17, the Apostle Paul speaks of "the revelation of the Lord Jesus from heaven *with the angels of his power* in flaming fire." When Jesus came the first time, He came as a babe wrapped in swaddling clothes and laid in a manger; He was despised and rejected of men; they did what they pleased with Him; the Divine glory was hidden beneath the veil of flesh; but when He comes again, His Divine glory and power will be manifest to every eye. As in His pre-existent state in the heavenly world, He was manifested to all the angelic world "in the *form* of God" (Phil. 2:6), so shall He be manifested to us. While He shall still be the Son of Man, He shall be Man wearing the very form of God, clothed with the outwardly manifest glory of God.

VI. *The coming of our Lord Jesus will be* SUDDEN AND UNANNOUNCED. He will come unexpectedly and without warning. He says in Rev. 16:15, "Behold, I come as a thief. Blessed is he that watcheth, and keepeth his garments, lest he walk naked, and they see his shame." This is constantly taken to refer to His coming at death, but the context and parallel passages show clearly that this is not the thought. In I Thess. 5:2, 3, the Holy Spirit speaking through the Apostle Paul says to the believers in Thessalonica, "For yourselves know perfectly that the day of the Lord so cometh *as a thief in the night.* When they are saying, Peace and safety, then sudden destruction cometh upon them, as travail upon a woman with child; and they shall in no wise escape." The Lord will not find when He comes again an expectant world, but an unexpectant world. The world will be taken up with its usual occupations; "And as were the days of Noah, so shall be the coming of the Son of Man. For as in those days which were before the flood they were eating and drinking, marrying and giving in marriage, until the day that Noah entered into the ark, and they knew not until the flood came, and took them all away; so shall be the coming of the Son of Man" (Matt. 24:37-39, R. V). Men and women will not be gathered on hilltops with white robes waiting for the descent of their Lord—everything will be going on just as usual and without any announcement, without any previous warning, unexpectedly and suddenly the trump of God shall sound; "for the Lord Himself shall descend from heaven with a shout, with the voice of the archangel, and with the trump of God." The attempt that so many are making to lay out a complete and very definite chart of events leading up to our Lord's Return loses sight of this clearly revealed fact about His coming. That He is coming we may be sure, but of every definite detail regarding His coming we cannot be sure. As the thief never sends word beforehand that He is coming, so our Lord will come without previous announcement. Our part is to be ready always, "For in an hour that ye think not the Son of Man cometh" (Matt. 24:44, R. V., cf. V. 43). We should always see to it that that day does not come upon us as a snare. How earnestly our Lord pleads with us, "Take heed to yourselves, lest haply your hearts be overcharged with surfeiting, and drunkenness, and cares of this life, and that day come on you suddenly as a snare: for so shall it come upon all them that dwell on the face of all the earth. But watch ye *at every season,* making supplication, that ye may prevail to escape all these things that shall come to pass, and to stand before the Son of Man" (Luke 21:34-36).

Chapter IV.

THE RESULTS OE THE RETURN OF OUR LORD JESUS.

The Results: As regards God—As regards the Church and individual believers—As regards Israel—As regards the Nations—As regards human society as a whole—As regards Anti-christ and the Devil—As regards the physical universe.

"Repent ye, therefore, and turn again, that your sins may be blotted out, that so there may come seasons of refreshing from the presence of the Lord; and that He may send the Christ who hath been appointed for you, even Jesus: whom the heavens must receive until the time of the restoration of all things, whereof God spoke by the mouth of His holy prophets that have been from of old."

ACTS 3:19-21.

CHAPTER IV

THE RESULTS OF THE RETURN OF OUR LORD JESUS

WE come now to the brightest, gladdest part of our whole study. The results of our Lord's Return to this earth as revealed in His Word are such that the very contemplation of them will fill the believer's heart not only with hope and longing but with gladness and ecstacy. These results are manifold. They may be classified under seven heads.

First, The results of The Return of our Lord Jesus, as regards God.

Second, The results as regards the Church and individual believers.

Third, The results as regards Israel.

Fourth, The results as regards the Nations.

Fifth, The results as regards human society as a whole.

Sixth, The results as regards the Antichrist and the Devil.

Seventh, The results as regards the physical universe.

I

The Results of the Return of our Lord Jesus as regards God.

1. The first result of the return of our Lord will be new glory to God. We read in Is. 40:5, R. V., "*The glory of Jehovah shall be revealed,* and all flesh shall see it together." The context clearly shows that it is at the coming of the Lord that this prophecy is to be fulfilled (see vs. 3, 9, 10). The glory of God has already been revealed in creation (Ps. 19:1); it is being revealed from century to century in history; it was revealed in the Person and work of Jesus Christ at His first coming; but the full revelation of the glory of God will be in connection with Christ's Second Coming. That is the first reason why we should desire it, that there may be new glory to the name of Him Whom we love and worship.

2. The second result of our Lord's Return is that He Himself will reign as a King. This we are told over and over again in the New Testament and in the Old. In the par-

able of the pounds our Lord compares Himself to "a certain nobleman (who) went into a far country *to receive for himself a kingdom* and to return" (Luke 19:12), and in the 15th verse He says, "And it came to pass when he was come back again, *having received the kingdom.*" He says again in Matt. 25:31, "When the Son of man shall come in His glory, and all the angels with Him, *then shall he sit on the throne of his glory.*" We find this representation of our Lord Jesus reigning as a King over and over again in the Old Testament. For example, in Jer. 23:5, 6, we read, "Behold, the days come, saith Jehovah, that I will raise unto David a righteous Branch, and he shall *reign as king and deal wisely,* and shall execute justice and righteousness in the land. In his days Judah shall be saved, and Israel shall dwell safely; and this is his name whereby he shall be called: Jehovah our righteousness." Referring to the same period, Jehovah declares in Ps. 2:6, "Yet *I have set my king* upon my holy hill of Zion." The Spirit of God through the prophet Zechariah sets forth the same truth in a way that emphasizes the Deity of our Lord. "*And Jehovah shall be king* over all the earth, and in that day shall Jehovah be one and His name one." The last book in the Bible returns to this reign of Christ again and again. For example in Rev. 19:11-16, we read, "And I saw the heaven opened; and behold, a white horse, and he that sat thereon called Faithful and True; and in righteousness he doth judge and make war. And his eyes are as a flame of fire, and upon his head are many diadems; and he hath a name written which no one knoweth but himself. And he is arrayed in a garment sprinkled with blood; and his name is called The Word of God. And the armies which are in heaven followed him upon white horses, clothed in fine linen, white and pure. And out of his mouth proceedeth a sharp sword, that with it he should smite the nations; and he shall rule them with a rod of iron; and he treadeth the winepress of the fierceness of the wrath of God, the Almighty. And he hath on his garment and on his thigh a name written, KING OF KINGS AND LORD OF LORDS." And again it is written in Rev. 20:4, "And I saw thrones, and they sat upon them, and judgment was given unto them; and I saw the souls of them that had been beheaded for the testimony of Jesus, and for the word of God, and such as worshipped not the beast, neither his image, and received not the mark upon their forehead and upon their hand; *and they lived and reigned with Christ* a thousand years." Yes, it is clearly revealed in the Word of God that the time is coming when our Lord Jesus, who was once despised and rejected of men, is to be acknowledged as King and is to rule here on the earth. The time is fast hastening on when the angel will sound his trumpet and there shall be great voices in heaven saying, "The kingdom of the world is become *the kingdom of our Lord and of His Christ,* and *He shall reign* forever and ever." The character and results of this blessed reign of our Lord, we shall consider later when we come to consider the results of His coming as regards Israel and human society as a whole.

II.

The Results of the Return of our Lord as regards the Church and individual believers.

1. The first result of the return of our Lord as regards believers is that immediately upon His coming in the air, THOSE WHO HAVE FALLEN ASLEEP IN HIM SHALL RISE. "For this we say unto you by the word of the Lord, that we that are alive, that are left unto the

coming of the Lord, shall in no wise precede them that are fallen asleep. For the Lord Himself shall descend from heaven, with a shout, with the voice of the archangel, and with the trump of God; and the *dead in Christ shall rise first*'' (I Thess. 4:15, 16 R. V). Until our Lord comes the bodies of those believers who have passed out of this world before that great event ''sleep in the dust of the earth'' (Dan. 12:2), their spirits are unclothed (II Cor. 5:4), they are ''absent from the body'' and ''at home with the Lord'' (II Cor. 5:4, 8). But immediately upon the sounding of the trump of God and the accompanying descent of our Lord, these bodies that sleep in the dust of the earth, are raised and the spirits of believers are no longer unclothed, ''but clothed upon with our habitation which is from heaven'' (II Cor. 5:2-4).

2. Following immediately upon the resurrection of the dead in Christ, THE BODIES OF LIVING BELIEVERS SHALL BE CHANGED FROM THEIR PRESENT STATE OF HUMILIATION INTO THE LIKENESS OF THE BODY OF HIS GLORY. The bodies that we now have are not the bodies that we shall have, ''We wait

for a Saviour, *the Lord Jesus Christ*: who shall *fashion anew the body of our humiliation, that it may be conformed to the body of his glory,* according to the working whereby he is able even to subject all things unto himself'' (Phil. 3:21). It is then and only then, that we are fully manifested outwardly as sons of God. We cannot but feel the limitations of our present bodies, as good as they are for many purposes, and we often groan within ourselves ''waiting for our adoption, to wit, the redemption of our body'' (Rom. 8:23). The redempton of our body comes when He comes, then the work of redemption is completed. We shall have a body like unto His own glorious body. This body will be incorruptible, not subject to decay, imperishable, glorious, powerful (I Cor. 15:42, 43). Our days of weariness and weakness will be forever at an end, the body will be able to accomplish all that the spirit purposes. It will be free from all the limitations of earth, and clothed upon with all the glory and power that pertains to the heavenly world. In a word, it will be a ''heavenly body'' (I Cor. 15:47-49). Our very bodies shall be luminous, shining, dazzling, bright like the sun. This is not imagination and poetry, but revealed fact. Our Lord says in Matt. 13:43, "*Then shall the righteous shine forth as the sun* in the kingdom of their father." This is not a part of the figurative language of the parable, but a part of the literal language of the interpretation of the parable. In a similar way centuries before it had been revealed by Jehovah to Daniel, "They that are wise *shall shine as the brightness of the firmament,* and they that turn many to righteousness *as the stars* forever and ever" (Dan. 12:3). When Jesus on the Mount of Transfiguration was being glorified before His disciples, *His face did shine as the sun,* and His garments became white as light (Matt. 7:2, cf Luke 9:29), and our bodies are to be like His. We shall no longer be subject to death, even the death of the body, but shall be like the angels (Luke 20:35, 36). This resurrection body will be the consummation of our adoption, our placing as sons. In the resurrection body then received, it will be outwardly manifest that we are sons of God. Before His incarnation, Christ was "*in the form of God*" (Phil. 2:6), that is, in the visible appearance of God and so shall we be in our resurrection bodies at His coming again.

3. The dead in Christ having been raised and the bodies of living believers having been transformed, THEY SHALL BOTH BE CAUGHT UP TOGETHER TO MEET THE LORD IN THE AIR, AND SO SHALL WE EVER BE WITH THE LORD (1 Thess. 4:17). It is especially to receive us unto Himself that Jesus Christ comes again at all. This He declared to His disciples on the night before He left them. He said, "If I go and prepare a place for you, I will come again and receive you unto myself, that where I am there ye may be also" (John 14:3). It is primarily love to His own that draws our Lord Jesus back to this earth again. He so loves us that he cannot get on without us. He sends no mere messenger for us, He comes Himself: "I come again" are His thrilling words. And it is to receive us "unto *Himself*" that He comes, not merely into heaven, but UNTO HIMSELF. The words indicate His intense longing for us, how He longs to press us to His very soul, His very self. We long for Him during His absence from us, but not as He longs for us. Even heaven itself is a lonely place to Him without us. Earth ought to be a lonely place to us without Him. Godet's comment on these words is worth repeating. Speaking of the believer and Christ's

attitude toward Him, he says, "He presses him to His heart, so to speak, while bearing him away. There is an infinite tenderness in these last words, 'unto myself.' It is for Himself that He seems to rejoice and look to this moment which will be the end of all separation."

4. At the coming again of our Lord Jesus and as a result of our then beholding Him as He is, WE SHALL BE MADE LIKE HIM. One of the most marvelous promises in the whole Bible is that uttered by John, the beloved disciple in I John 3:2. He says, "Beloved, now are we the children of God, and it is not yet made manifest what we shall be. We know that if He shall be manifested, *we shall be like Him;* for we shall see Him even as He is." The perfect beholding of our Lord in that day shall transform us into the perfect image of the Lord whom we behold. Even in the life that now is, it is through beholding the glory of the Lord that we are "transformed into the same image from glory to glory," that is, each new view of Him imparts something more of His glory to us. But now we see only through a glass darkly and consequently our reflection of His glory is imperfect. Then we shall see Him face to face

in His undimmed glory and shall perfectly reflect it. Our Lord then, when we are transformed into His perfect likeness, spiritually as well as bodily, shall be "glorified *in* His saints," not merely glorified by us but glorified in us. His glory shall be fully revealed in what we are in that day (II Thess. 1:10). Not only shall He be manifested in all the fullness of His glory, but we also together with Him shall be "manifested in glory" (Col. 3:4, R. V). Oftentimes, when laboring to uplift those who have fallen deeply into sin, and whose character has been so disfigured by the wicked life that they have led that the process of salvation has been hindered by many a discouraging fall, and I have felt tempted to give up the battle for their redemption, I have taken new courage as I have thought of I John 3:2, and have said to myself, "though this one you are trying to save now seems so little like the Lord that it seems a waste of time to do anything more to help him, still some day, when our Lord comes and he gets one glimpse of Him as He is, he shall be transformed into His perfect image that he shall be just like Him." And oftentimes when discouraged over my own failures, and almost overwhelmed with the thought of how unlike I was to my Master, the glad thought has thrilled me that it will not always be so, but some day, that glad day when the Lord Himself shall descend from heaven with a shout, with the voice of the archangel, and the trump of God, and I am caught up to meet Him, and when I see Him as He is, I too will be just like Him, in all the infinite perfection of His character, then shall I "attain unto the measure of the stature of the fullness of Christ."

5. And now a still more wonderful result follows, OUR LORD JESUS WILL BE UNITED IN MARRIAGE WITH THE CHURCH, HIS BETROTHED BRIDE (cf Eph. 5:23, 32), and the marriage supper of the Lamb be celebrated. John says, "And I heard as it were the voice of a great multitude, and as the voice of many waters, and as the voice of many thunders, saying, Hallelujah; for the Lord our God, the Almighty, reigneth. Let us rejoice and be exceeding glad, and let us give the glory unto Him: for the *marriage of the Lamb is come* and his wife hath made herself ready. And it was given unto her that she should array herself in fine linen, bright and pure: for the fine linen is the righteous acts of the

saints. And he saith unto me, Write, Blessed are they that are bidden to the marriage supper of the Lamb'' (Rev. 19:6-9). These words are so remarkable that it is no wonder that the angel who spoke them to John felt the necessity of adding, ''These are true words of God.'' All the depth of meaning that there is in them, it is impossible for us now to fathom, and this is a place where speculation should be very guarded; but this much has been revealed, that in Christ in His relation to His church, and there alone, has the full significance of marriage been realized (Eph. 5:31, 32), and that this intimate relation between Christ and His Church will be fully realized at His Coming Again.

6. At the return of our Lord EACH ONE OF HIS SERVANTS SHALL RECEIVE HIS REWARD: ''For the Son of man shall come in the glory of His Father with his angels; and *then shall he render unto every man according to his deeds''* (Matt. 16:27). It is not at death but at the coming of the Lord that we receive our full reward. All of those who love His appearing shall receive a crown of righteousness. It was in anticipation of this that Paul, as he sat in his prison cell in Rome awaiting execution, wrote, ''I have fought the good

fight, I have finished the course, I have kept the faith: henceforth there is laid up for me *the crown of righteousness,* which the Lord the righteous judge, shall give me *at that day*: and not to me only, but also to all them that loved his appearing" (II Tim. 4:7-8). The faithful shepherds of the flock shall receive a crown of glory that fadeth not away. It was with this in view that the Apostle Peter exhorted elders to "Tend the flock of God which is among you, exercising the oversight, not of constraint, but willingly, according to the will of God; nor yet for filthy lucre, but of a ready mind; neither as lording it over the charge allotted to you, but making yourselves ensamples to the flock. And *when the chief Shepherd shall be manifested, ye shall receive the crown of glory that fadeth not away*" (I Pet. 5:2-4).

7. When our Lord returns, HIS PEOPLE SHALL LIVE AND REIGN WITH HIM. John says, "And I saw thrones, and they sat upon them, and judgment was given unto them; and I saw the souls of them that had been beheaded for the testimony of Jesus, and for the word of God, and such as worshipped not the beast, neither His image, and received not the mark upon their forehead and upon

their hand; *and they lived, and reigned with Christ a thousand years"* (Rev. 20:4). This passage seems to refer primarily to the tribulation saints, but by implication it includes all those who have believed in Jesus in this present dispensation. Certainly the Bride must reign with her Husband, and we are explicitly told in Rev. 5:9, 10, that our Lord has made those whom He purchased of every tribe and tongue and people and nation to be a kingdom unto God and priests and that they shall *"reign upon the earth."*

III.

The Results of the Return of our Lord as regards Israel.

1. There shall be great joy among His people Israel because of our Lord's Return. The prophet Isaiah, speaking of that day says, "It shall be said in that day, Lo this is our God, we have waited for Him and He will save us; This is Jehovah, We have waited for Him. We will be glad and rejoice in his salvation." This can hardly be limited to Israel, but the context seems to clearly imply that the primary reference is to them. Why Israel shall rejoice will become evident enough as we study the further

results of His coming again. But as great as their joy shall be, it shall begin with a great mourning; mourning over their sin, and especially over their former rejection of their King. The prophet Zechariah tells us in Zech. 12:8-14, "In that day shall Jehovah defend the inhabitants of Jerusalem; and he that is feeble among them at that day shall be as David; and the house of David shall be as God, as the angel of Jehovah before them. And it shall come to pass in that day, that I will seek to destroy all the nations that come against Jerusalem. And I will pour upon the house of David, and upon the inhabitants of Jerusalem, the spirit of grace and of supplication; *and they shall look unto me whom they have pierced and they shall mourn for him,* as one mourneth for his only son, and shall be in bitterness for Him, as one that is in bitterness for his first-born. In that day shall there be a great mourning in Jerusalem, as the mourning of Hadadrimmon in the valley of Megiddon. And the land shall mourn, every family apart; the family of the house of David apart, and their wives apart; the family of the house of Nathan apart, and their wives apart; the family of the house of Levi apart, and their wives apart; the family of the house of the Shimeites apart, and their wives apart; all the families that remain, every family apart, and their wives apart." But following their mourning a fountain shall be opened for sin and for uncleanness (Zech. 13:1) and Jehovah Himself shall go forth to fight against all their enemies (Zech. 14:1-3).

2. Following upon what has just been said, THE RETURN OF OUR LORD JESUS SHALL RESULT IN ISRAEL'S DELIVERANCE IN THE DAY WHEN HIS TRIALS AND SUFFERINGS CULMINATE. We read in Zech. 14:1-4, "Behold, a day of Jehovah cometh when the spoil shall be divided in the midst of thee. For I will gather all nations against Jerusalem to battle; and the city shall be taken, and the houses rifled, and the women ravished; and half of the city shall go forth into captivity, and the residue of the people shall not be cut off from the city. *Then shall Jehovah go forth, and fight against those nations*: as when he fought in the days of battle. And his feet shall stand in that day upon the mount of Olives, which is before Jerusalem on the east; and the mount of Olives shall be cleft in the midst thereof toward the east and toward the west, and there shall be a very

great valley; and half of the mountain shall remove toward the north and half of it toward the south." History in our day seems to be fast heading up toward the day when these promises shall be fulfilled.

3. In connection with the Return of our Lord, THE CHILDREN OF ISRAEL SHALL BE GATHERED TOGETHER FROM AMONG THE NATIONS, FROM THE FOUR CORNERS OF THE EARTH AND BROUGHT AGAIN INTO THEIR OWN LAND. This is promised over and over again in the prophecies of the Old Testament. We read in Is. 11:11, 12, "And it shall come to pass in that day, that the Lord will set his hand again the second time to recover the remnant of his people, that shall remain, from Assyria, and from Egypt, and from Pathros, and from Cush, and from Elam, and from Shinar, and from Hamath, and from the Islands of the sea. And he will set up an ensign for the nations, and will assemble the outcasts of Israel, and gather together the dispersed of Judah from the four corners of the earth." In a similar way we read in Ezek. 36:24, "For I will take you from among the nations and gather you out of all the countries, and will bring you into your own land." And again in the 37th chapter, 21st verse,

"Thus saith the Lord Jehovah: Behold I will take the children of Israel from among the nations, whither they are gone, and will gather them on every side, and bring them into their own land." And in the prophecy of Zephaniah we also read, "Behold at that time I will deal with all them that afflict thee; and I will save that which is lame, and gather that which was driven away; and I will make them a praise and a name, whose shame had been in the earth. At that time will I bring you in, and at that time will I gather you; for I will make you a name and a praise among all the peoples of the earth, when I bring back your captivity before your eyes, saith Jehovah" (Zeph. 3:19, 20). These prophecies cannot refer to any return of Israel which has as yet taken place, but they will be fulfilled to the very letter in connection with the Second Coming of Christ.

4. At the time of our Lord's Return EPHRAIM *and* JUDAH WHO HAVE BEEN SO LONG DIVIDED ONE FROM THE OTHER, SHALL BE UNITED IN ONE NATION UNDER ONE KING, DAVID. This is made very plain in Ezek. 37:19, 22, 24, "Thus saith the Lord Jehovah: Behold I will take the stick of Joseph which is in the hand of Ephraim, and the tribes of Israel,

his companions; and I will put them with it, even with the stick of Judah, and make them one stick, and they shall be one in my hand. . . . . And I will make them one nation in the land, upon the mountains of Israel; and one king shall be king to them all; and they shall be no more two nations, neither shall they be divided into two kingdoms any more at all. . . . . And my servant David shall be king over them; and they all shall have one shepherd; and they shall also walk in mine ordinances, and observe my statutes, and do them."

5. Closely connected with what has just been said, it is revealed in God's Word that because of our Lord's Return, JUDAH SHALL BE SAVED AND ISRAEL SHALL DWELL SAFELY. "Behold, the days come, saith Jehovah, that I will raise unto David a righteous Branch, and he shall reign as king and deal wisely, and shall execute justice and righteousness in the land. *In his days Judah shall be saved, and Israel shall dwell safely*" (Jer. 23:5, 6). There shall be a national salvation of all Israelites then upon the earth. As Paul puts it, "And so *all Israel shall be saved;* even as it is written, There shall come out of Zion a Deliverer; He shall turn away ungodliness

from Jacob; and this is my covenant unto them, when I shall take away their sins" (Rom. 11:26, 27). "The gifts and the calling of God are not repented of", and though Israel has proven untrue to the covenant of God, yet God remains faithful. At present they are enemies for our sake, but as touching the election they are beloved for the fathers' sake and in due time in connection with the Return of our Lord, God will have mercy upon them all (cf Rom. 11:28-32). Israel shall be cleansed from all their filthiness and from all their idols, a new heart will be given unto them, and a new spirit put within them, the stony heart shall be taken away from them and they shall be given a heart of flesh; God will put His Spirit within them and cause them to walk in His statutes, and they shall keep His judgments and do them. This in every detail is a matter of Divine prediction. Jehovah Himself says through the prophet Ezekiel, "Neither shall they defile themselves any more with their idols, nor with their detestable things, nor with any of their transgressions but I will save them out of all their dwelling places, wherein they have sinned, and will cleanse them; so shall they be my people, and I will be their God (Ezek. 37:23). In the preceding chapter Ezek. 36:25-27, He had already said, "I will sprinkle clean water upon you and ye shall be clean; from all your filthiness and from all your idols, will I cleanse you. A new heart also will I give you, and a new spirit will I put within you; and I will take away the stony heart out of your flesh, and I will give you a heart of flesh. And I will put my Spirit within you, and cause you to walk in my statutes, and ye shall keep my ordinances, and do them. . . . . And I will save you from all your uncleannesses; and I will call for the grain and multiply it, and lay no famine upon you." The same thought is expressed in other words through the Prophet Jeremiah where we read, "Behold, the days come, saith Jehovah, that I will make a new covenant with the house of Israel, and with the house of Judah; not according to the covenant that I made with their fathers in the day that I took them by the hand to bring them out of the land of Egypt; which my covenant they brake, although I was a husband unto them, saith Jehovah. But this is the covenant that I will make with the house of Israel after those days, saith Jehovah: I will put my law in their inward parts, and in their heart will I write it; and I will be their God and they shall be my people. And they shall teach no more every man his neighbor, and every man his brother, saying, Know Jehovah; for they shall all know me, from the least of them unto the greatest of them, saith Jehovah; for I will forgive their iniquity, and their sin will I remember no more" (Jer. 31:33-34).

6. Because of the Return of our Lord Jesus and the events spoken of above that grow out of that Return, ISRAEL SHALL BE WONDROUSLY MULTIPLIED AND THE WASTE, DESERT AND RUINED CITIES SHALL BE REBUILT AND THE NOW DESOLATE LAND BECOME LIKE THE GARDEN OF EDEN; JERUSALEM SHALL BE CALLED "THE CITY OF TRUTH" AND SHALL BE FILLED WITH PEACE, PROSPERITY, AND GLADNESS. The Old Testament Prophets abound with predictions of this golden age for Israel that is coming. In Ezek. 36:37-38, we read, "Thus saith the Lord Jehovah: for this, moreover, will I be inquired of by the house of Israel, to do it for them. I will increase them with men like a flock. As the flock for sacrifice and the flock of Jerusalem in her appointed feasts, so shall the waste cities be filled with

flocks of men; and they shall know that I am Jehovah.'' And in Jer. 31:27 we read, ''Behold the days come, saith Jehovah, that I will sow the house of Judah with the seed of men, and with the seed of beast.'' Turn again to Ezek. and we read in the 36th chapter and the 33rd to 36th verses, ''Thus saith the Lord Jehovah; in the day that I will cleanse you from all your iniquities, I will cause the cities to be inhabited, and the waste places shall be builded. And the land that was desolate shall be tilled, whereas it was a desolation in the sight of all that passed by. And they shall say, this land that was desolate is become like the garden of Eden; and the waste and desolate and ruined cities are fortified and inhabited. Then the nations that are left round about you shall know that I, Jehovah, have builded the ruined places, and planted that which was desolate. I Jehovah have spoken it, and I will do it.'' Zechariah also has his picture of the glad coming days when judgment shall be followed by blessing. In the 8th chapter, 3rd to 5th verses we read, ''Thus saith Jehovah: I am returned unto Zion, and will dwell in the midst of Jerusalem; and Jerusalem shall be called The city of truth; and the mountain of

Jehovah of hosts, The holy mountain. Thus saith Jehovah of hosts; There shall yet old men and old women dwell in the streets of Jerusalem, and every man with his staff in his hand for very age. And the streets of the city shall be full of boys and girls playing in the streets thereof.'' This is not, as it is so often taken to be, a picture of heaven, but a picture of the literal Jerusalem in the glad day that is coming as the outcome of the Return of our Lord to this earth. Israel in that day shall be greatly exalted above the nations. We read in the 23d verse of this same chapter, ''Thus saith Jehovah of hosts: In those days it shall come to pass, that ten men shall take hold, out of all the languages of the nations, they shall take hold of the skirt of him that is a Jew, saying, We will go with you, for we have heard that God is with you'' (Zech. 8:23). This same thought is more fully expressed in Is. 49:22-23, ''Thus saith the Lord Jehovah, Behold I will lift up my hand to the nations, and set up my ensign to the peoples; and they shall bring thy sons in their bosom, and thy daughters shall be carried upon their shoulders. And kings shall be thy nursing fathers, and their queens thy nursing mothers; they shall bow down to thee with their faces to the earth, and lick the dust of thy feet; and thou shalt know that I am Jehovah; and they that wait for me shall not be put to shame." It is very plain to anyone who will carefully read the chapter and note exactly what is said that this cannot refer to "the ample restoration of the Church," as some have interpreted it, but to the future glory of Israel, God's earthly people.

7. Having been restored and exalted above the nations, ISRAEL SHALL GO FORTH AS PREACHERS OF THE GLORY OF JEHOVAH TO ALL NATIONS.

In the last chapter of his prophecy, Isaiah represents Jehovah as saying, "And I will set a sign among them, and I will send such *as escape of them unto the nations,* to Tarshish, Pul, and Lud, that draw the bow, to Tubal and Javan, to the isles afar off, that have not heard my fame, neither have seen my glory; *and they shall declare my glory among the nations*" (Is. 66:19). Though the great mass of Israelites are today rejecting the Lord Jesus, they are still destined to become the greatest missionaries in the world's history. What one Jew, who had once bitterly opposed the Lord, did, after his conversion when he went out as the Apostle to the Gentiles (that is the nations) will give us some hint of what the whole people will do when they have been converted and go forth as missionaries in that great coming day.

IV.

The Results of the Return of our Lord as Regards the Nations and Unregenerate Individuals.

1. The first result of the Return of our Lord as regards the nations, that is to say, the other peoples of the earth except Israel, will be A UNIVERSAL MOURNING OVER HIM. We read in Rev. 1:7 R. V., "Behold He cometh with the clouds; and every eye shall see him, and they that pierced him; and all the *tribes of the earth shall mourn over him.*" Our Lord Jesus Himself declared the same fact. He said to His disciples in expounding to them the facts concerning His own coming, "And then shall appear the sign of the Son of man in heaven; and *then shall all the tribes of the earth mourn,* and they shall see the Son of man coming on the clouds of heaven with power and great glory" (Matt. 24:30, R. V.). The gladdest day of all for His people will be the saddest day of all for those who

are not His people. For His people it will be the consummation of all their hopes and longings, but for those who have rejected Him it will be the shattering of all their hopes and projects.

2. ALL THE NATIONS SHALL BE GATHERED BEFORE HIM FOR JUDGMENT AND HE SHALL SEPARATE THEM ONE FROM ANOTHER AS THE SHEPHERD DIVIDETH HIS SHEEP FROM HIS GOATS. The Lord Jesus says in Matt. 25:31-32, "But when the Son of man shall come in his glory, and all the angels with him, then shall he sit on the throne of his glory; *and before him shall be gathered all the nations; and he shall separate them one from another, as the shepherd separateth the sheep from the goats.*" Then shall follow the judgment of those nations then living on the earth—the sheep on His right hand shall go away into eternal life; and the goats on His left hand into eternal punishment. "Then shall the king say unto them on his right hand, Come, ye blessed of my Father, inherit the kingdom prepared for you from the foundation of the world; for I was hungry, and ye gave me to eat; I was thirsty, and ye gave me drink, I was a stranger and ye took me in; naked, and ye clothed me; I was sick and ye visited me; I

was in prison, and ye came unto me. Then shall the righteous answer him, saying, Lord, when saw we thee hungry, and fed thee? or athirst and gave thee drink? And when saw we thee a stranger, and took thee in? or naked, and clothed thee? And when saw we thee sick, or in prison, and came unto thee? And the king shall answer and say unto them, Verily I say unto you, Inasmuch as ye did it unto one of these my brethren, even these least, ye did it unto me. Then shall he say also unto them on the left hand, Depart from me ye cursed, into the eternal fire which is prepared for the devil and his angels; for I was hungry, and ye did not give me to eat; I was thirsty, and ye gave me no drink; I was a stranger, and ye took me not in; naked, and ye clothed me not; sick, and in prison, and ye visited me not. Then shall they also answer, saying, Lord, when saw we thee hungry, or athirst, or a stranger, or naked, or sick, or in prison, and did not minister to thee? Then shall he answer them, saying, Verily I say unto you, Inasmuch as ye did it not unto one of these least, ye did it not unto me. And these shall go away into eternal punishment; but the righteous into eternal life" (Matt. 25:34-46).

3. At the Return of Our Lord Jesus, ALL THE GENTILES UPON WHOM HIS NAME IS CALLED WILL SEEK AFTER THE LORD. "After these things I will return, and I will build again the tabernacle of David which is fallen; and I will build again the ruins thereof, and I will set it up; That the residue of men may seek after the Lord, and all the Gentiles, upon whom my name is called" (Acts 15:16-17). "Yea, many peoples and strong nations shall come to seek Jehovah of hosts in Jerusalem, and to entreat the favor of Jehovah." (Zech. 8:22). There will be a great turning unto the Lord. "And it shall come to pass in the latter days, that the mountain of Jehovah's house shall be established on the top of the mountains, and shall be exalted above the hills; and all nations shall flow into it. And many peoples shall go and say, Come ye, and let us go up to the mountain of Jehovah to the house of the God of Jacob; and he will teach us his ways, and we will walk in his paths; for out of Zion shall go forth the law, and the word of Jehovah from Jerusalem" (Is. 2:2, 3). The question will naturally arise here, how can this be, if immediately upon His coming, the nations are gathered before Him, judged, separated and assigned to their eter-

nal destiny? The answer is very simple. It is nowhere said that *immediately upon His coming* the nations will be gathered, judged, separated and assigned to their eternal destiny. Our difficulty here, as in many other places, arises from the fact that we assume what the Bible never asserts nor implies, viz, that these things are all crowded into a day, or a few days or even a year. All these events are connected with and result from His coming, but they take time for their development. Prophecies are never intended to give us the definite and detailed history in their order of all the events connected with the Lord's coming. It is never the method of prophecy to give a definite and detailed history in their order of all the events connected with the subject in hand. The great important facts necessary to keep us watching and to cheer our hearts and fire us for our work are given in outline, but we should always bear in mind that while prophecy is exactly and literally true in every word, and will be exactly and literally fulfilled, that nevertheless, prophecy is not history.

4. As a result of the Return of our Lord Jesus and of His glorious reign that follows

that Return, ALL THOSE WHO ARE REBELLIOUS AGAINST HIM WILL BE SHATTERED. "Thou shalt break them," says the Holy Spirit through the Psalmist, "with a rod of iron. Thou shalt dash them in pieces like a potter's vessel" (Ps. 2:9, note the context). Our Lord will "execute judgment upon all, and convict all the ungodly of all their works of ungodliness which they have ungodly wrought, and of all the hard things which ungodly sinners have spoken against him" (Jude 15). He will "punish the inhabitants of the earth for their iniquity" (Is. 26-21). "He will render vengeance to them that know not God, and to them that obey not the Gospel of our Lord Jesus; who shall suffer punishment, even eternal destruction from the face of the Lord and from the glory of his might" (II Thess. 1:8, 9). As to what destruction means in this passage, we learn from a comparison of Rev. 17:11 with Rev. 20:10, and Rev. 19:20. In Rev. 17:11 we are told the beast "goeth into *perdition.*" The word here translated "perdition" is the same Greek word which is elsewhere translated "destruction" and might well have been so translated here and thus have avoided confusion. If we can find where the beast goes, we will then know what "perdition" or "destruction" means. In Rev. 19:20 we have a very explicit statement of where the "beast goeth." We are here told that "the beast was taken and with him the false prophet that wrought the signs in his sight, wherewith he deceived them that had received the mark of the beast and them that worshipped his image; they two were cast alive into the lake of fire that burneth with brimstone." But what becomes of the beast in that lake of fire? Is he annihilated? Does he lose conscious existence? This question is answered in the 10th verse of the following chapter (Rev. 20:10): "And the devil that deceived them was cast into the lake of fire and brimstone, where *are* also the beast and the false prophet." Let us remember that this is after the thousand years and we see that the beast and the false prophet *are* still there. They have not been consumed in the sense of ceasing to be in the thousand years that have elapsed since they were put there, and we are furthermore told in the remainder of the verse, "They shall be tormented day and night forever and ever." The words translated "they shall be tormented" in this passage can only refer to conscious torment, so God's own definition of destruction is "a condition of conscious and awful torment."

5. But there is a bright side to the results of our Lord's coming even in regard to the nations. It is clearly taught that EVERY ONE THAT IS LEFT OF THE NATIONS AND KINGS AND PRINCES SHALL WORSHIP AND SERVE JESUS CHRIST. We read in Zech. 14:16, "And it shall come to pass, that every one that is left of all the nations that come against Jerusalem shall go up from year to year to worship the King, Jehovah of hosts, and to keep the feast of tabernacles." And in Is. 49:7 we read, "Thus saith Jehovah, the Redeemer of Israel, and His Holy One, to him whom man despiseth, to him whom the nation abhorreth, to a servant of rulers; Kings shall see and arise; princes, and they shall worship; because of Jehovah that is faithful, even the Holy One of Israel, who hath chosen thee." That this refers to the kings and princes of the Gentiles is evident from the verse that immediately precedes, "I will also give thee for a light to the Gentiles, that thou mayest be my salvation unto the end of the earth." Along the same line in Rev. 15:4 we read, "Who shall not fear, O Lord, and glorify thy name? for thou only art holy; for all the

nations shall come and worship before thee." And in the wonderful prophecy concerning our Lord found in the 2nd Psalm we read in the 8th verse, "Ask of me, and I will give thee *the nations* for thine inheritance, and the uttermost parts of the earth for thy possession." And in that other marvelous prophetic picture of the Lord Jesus in the 72nd Psalm, the 8th to the 11th verses, we read, "He shall have dominion from sea to sea, and from the River unto the ends of the earth. They that dwell in the wilderness shall bow before him; and his enemies shall lick the dust. The kings of Tarshish and of the isles shall render tribute; the kings of Sheba and Seba shall offer gifts. Yea, all kings shall fall down before him; all nations shall serve him." "He shall speak peace unto the nations; and his dominion shall be from sea to sea, and from the River unto the ends of the earth" (Zech. 9:10). To sum it all up, "The kingdom of the world" shall "become the kingdom of our Lord and of his Christ; and he shall reign forever and ever" (Rev. 11:15.)

V.

The Results of the Return of our Lord Jesus as regards human society as a whole.

At the Return of our Lord Jesus and as a result of that return, WAR SHALL CEASE, PEACE AND PLENTY SHALL REIGN AND THE RIGHTEOUS SHALL FLOURISH. This is declared over and over again in the prophetic Scriptures. For example, we read in Is. 2:2, 4, "And it shall come to pass in the latter days, that the mountain of Jehovah's house shall be established on the top of the mountains, and shall be exalted above the hills; and all nations shall flow unto it. And he will judge between the nations, and will decide concerning many peoples; and they shall beat their swords into plowshares, and their spears into pruning hooks; nation shall not lift up sword against nation, neither shall they learn war any more." We find a similar picture of those glad coming days in the prophecy of Micah: "And he will judge between many peoples, and will decide concerning strong nations afar off; and they shall beat their swords into ploughshares, and their spears into pruning hooks; nation shall not lift up sword against nation, neither shall they learn war any more. But they shall sit every man under his vine and under his fig-tree; and none shall make them afraid; for the mouth of Jehovah of hosts hath spoken it'' (Micah 4:3, 4). Then and only then will be realized what the greatest statesmen of the present day are trying to work out. Now we have our ''Peace Conferences'' and our gatherings at The Hague, and they have accomplished something, but they will prove utterly futile to accomplish all that is in the mind and heart of our greatest statesmen. While we talk peace, we are increasing our navies and our armies. We are squandering untold millions in schemes for destroying the lives of our fellow men and for the protection and extension of our own nation. We talk of disarmament, but we all know it is not coming. All our present peace plans will end in the most awful wars and conflicts this old world ever saw, but none the less there is a good day coming when war shall be at an end, when there shall be universal peace, when there shall no longer be conflict between nation and nation, nor between class and class, when there will be no more strikes, because strikes will not be needed; when industrial wars, as well as wars between nations, will be over and peace and plenty shall reign; when the prophetic vision of the Psalmist will be realized, ''In his days shall the righteous flourish, and abundance of peace, till the moon be no more. There shall be abundance of grain in the earth upon the top of the mountains'' (Ps. 72:7, 16). All this is to be realized at and as a result of the Return of our Lord Jesus.

2. THE WHOLE EARTH SHALL BE FULL OF THE KNOWLEDGE OF THE LORD. This, too, is clearly proclaimed by God through His prophet Isaiah. We read in Is. 11:2-5, ''And there shall come forth a shoot out of the stock of Jesse, and a branch out of his roots shall bear fruit. And the Spirit of Jehovah shall rest upon him, the spirit of wisdom and understanding, the spirit of counsel and might, the spirit of knowledge and of the fear of Jehovah. And his delight shall be in the fear of Jehovah; and he shall not judge after the sight of his eyes, neither decide after the hearing of his ears; but with righteousness shall he judge the poor, and decide with equity for the meek of the earth; and he shall smite the earth with the rod of his mouth; and with the breath of his lips shall he slay the wicked. And righteousness shall be the girdle of his waist, and faithfulness the girdle of his loins. They shall not hurt nor destroy in all my holy mountain;

for *the earth shall be full of the knowledge of Jehovah, as the waters cover the sea.*" The Utopia of which poets and philosophers and romancers and statesmen have dreamed will become a reality. It will not be realized through any of our modern sociological schemes. One social theory after another is brought forward that promises much, but they all end in failure, and they all will end in failure until our Lord comes. Their aim is good but their method is always impracticable. But the day of Christ's Coming Again and reigning will realize everything that men have striven for in these directions. It will be the golden age of the earth and we may well cry, as did John of old, "Amen; Come, Lord Jesus."

VI.

The Results of the Return of our Lord Jesus as Regards the Antichrist and the Devil.

As a result of the return of our Lord Jesus, THE ANTICHRIST SHALL BE PUT OUT OF THE WAY. As the Holy Spirit puts it through the Apostle Paul in II Thess. 2:3, 4, 7, 8, "Let no man beguile you in any wise; for it will not be, except the falling away come first, and the man of sin be revealed, the son of perdition, he that opposeth and exalteth himself against all that is called God or that is worshipped; so that he sitteth in the temple of God, setting himself forth as God. . . . For the mystery of lawlessness doth already work; only there is one that restraineth now, until he be taken out of the way. And then shall be revealed the lawless one, *whom the Lord Jesus shall slay* (or, "put out of the way" cf Rev. 19:20) with the breath of his mouth, and bring to naught by the manifestation of his coming." It is clearly revealed in the Word of God that there is a mighty king coming to this earth, the personal representative of Satan, who shall gain great power and dominion throughout the Roman world. The days of his reign are to be awful days, but the days of his reign will be brief and his overthrow overwhelming.

2. THE DEVIL HIMSELF SHALL BE CHAINED AND CAST INTO THE ABYSS FOR A THOUSAND YEARS, AND THEN AFTER A LITTLE SPACE OF LIBERTY HE SHALL BE CAST INTO THE LAKE OF FIRE, WHERE HE SHALL BE TORMENTED DAY AND NIGHT FOREVER AND EVER. This, too, is clearly

revealed in the Word of God. We read in Rev. 20:1-3, "And I saw an angel coming down out of heaven, having the key of the abyss and a great chain in his hand. And he laid hold on the dragon, the old serpent, which is the Devil and Satan, and bound him for a thousand years, and cast him into the abyss, and shut it and sealed it over him, that he should deceive the nations no more, until the thousand years should be finished; after this he must be loosed for a little time." Then follows a brief account of the thousand years. Then we read again in the 7th to the 10th verses, "And when the thousand years are finished Satan shall be loosed out of his prison, and shall come forth to deceive the nations which are in the four corners of the earth, Gog and Magog, to gather them together to the war; the number of whom is as the sand of the sea. And they compassed the camp of the saints about, and the beloved city; and fire came down out of heaven, and devoured them. And the Devil that deceived them was cast into the lake of fire and brimstone, where are also the beast and the false prophet; and they shall be tormented day and night forever and ever."

VII.

The Results of the Return of our Lord Jesus as Regards the Physical Universe.

The coming again of our Lord has results not only as regards man but as regards the physical universe as well.

1. In connection with Christ's coming again and as a result of it, THE CREATION ITSELF SHALL BE DELIVERED FROM THE BONDAGE OF CORRUPTION TO WHICH IT IS NOW SUBJECT INTO THE LIBERTY OF THE GLORY OF THE CHILDREN OF GOD. Thorns and briars and carnage shall be no more. Even the wilderness and solitary place and the desert shall rejoice and blossom as the rose. This is revealed in both the Old Testament and the New. The Apostle Paul wrote in Rom. 8:19-21, "For the earnest expectation of the creation waiteth for the revealing of the sons of God. For the creation was subjected to vanity, not of its own will, but by reason of him who subjected it, in hope that the creation itself also shall be delivered from the bondage of corruption into the liberty of the glory of the children of God." Everywhere in nature now we find pain and suffering, disease and death. Much of the music of the

insects that we hear in the air is not a song of joy but the sound of pain, but the glad day is coming when pain and disease and death will cease among the lower orders of creation as well as among men. Nature fell in connection with the fall of man, the head of the earthly creation, and in his redemption the creation shall be redeemed also, and this will be fulfilled in connection with the coming of Christ. The prophet Isaiah says in Is. 55:13, "Instead of the thorn shall come up the fir-tree; and instead of the brier shall come up the myrtle-tree; and it shall be to Jehovah for a name, for an everlasting sign that shall not be cut off." This is not poetry and figure but the revelation of literal facts that shall take place upon this earth. Again Isaiah says in Is. 65:25, "The wolf and the lamb shall feed together, and the lion shall eat straw like an ox; and dust shall be the serpent's food. They shall not hurt nor destroy in all my holy mountain, saith Jehovah." The carniverous beast shall be changed—not even the wolf will destroy the lamb—they shall both feed on the grass. Again Isaiah says, "The wilderness (shall) become a fruitful field, and the fruitful field be esteemed a forest"

(Is. 32:15). And once more we read, "The wilderness and the dry land shall be glad; and the desert shall rejoice, and blossom as the rose. It shall blossom abundantly, and rejoice even with joy and singing; the glory of Lebanon shall be given unto it, the excellency of Carmel and Sharon; they shall see the glory of Jehovah, the excellency of our God" (Is. 35:1, 2). The most desolate parts of the earth shall become more beautiful and fruitful than the most fertile portions of the earth are to-day.

2. Bright as the foregoing picture is, even a better day is coming—THERE SHALL BE A NEW HEAVEN AND A NEW EARTH. We read in II Pet. 3:12, 13, "Looking for and earnestly desiring the coming of the day of God, by reason of which the heavens being on fire shall be dissolved, and the elements shall melt with fervent heat. But according to his promise, we LOOK FOR NEW HEAVENS AND A NEW EARTH, Wherein dwelleth righteousness." We see a picture of the fulfillment of this prophecy in Rev. 21:1-5, "And I saw a new heaven and a new earth; for the first heaven and the first earth are passed away; and the sea is no more. And I saw the holy city, new Jerusalem, coming

down out of heaven from God, made ready as a bride adorned for her husband. And I heard a great voice out of the throne saying, Behold the tabernacle of God is with men, and he shall dwell with them, and they shall be his people, and God himself shall be with them, and be their God; and he shall wipe away every tear from their eyes; and death shall be no more; neither shall there be mourning, nor crying, nor pain any more; the first things are passed away. And he that sitteth on the throne said, Behold I make all things new. And he saith, Write; for these words are faithful and true."

To sum it all up, AS THE RESULT OF OUR LORD'S RETURN, THERE WILL BE A NEW AND GLORIOUS MAN, IN A NEW AND GLORIOUS BODY, IN A NEW AND GLORIOUS SOCIETY, IN A NEW AND GLORIOUS UNIVERSE. "Amen; *Come, Lord Jesus.*"

Chapter V.

THE TIME OF OUR LORD'S RETURN.

It is unknown—No definite date revealed—It will be when men think not—When the world will be absorbed in its pursuits—After the revelation of the Man of Sin—In a time of apostasy —So far as we know, at any moment.

"It is not for you to know times or seasons which the Father hath set within His own authority."

ACTS 2:7.

"But forget not this one thing, beloved, that one day is with the Lord as a thousand years, and a thousand years as one day."

2 PETER 3:8.

"Watch, therefore: for ye know not when the master of the house cometh, whether at even, or at midnight, or at the cockcrowing, or in the morning; lest coming suddenly he find you sleeping. And what I say unto you I say unto all, Watch."

MARK 13:35-37.

CHAPTER V.

THE TIME OF OUR LORD'S RETURN

OVER and over again we are told in the Word of God that *the exact time of our Lord's return is not known, and cannot be known, by man.* Our Lord Jesus Himself declares in Matt. 24:35, "But of that day and hour knoweth no one, not even the angels of heaven, neither the Son, but *the Father only.*" And on the ground of this fact that we do not know the exact time of our Lord's return He says, "Watch therefore; for ye know not on what day your Lord cometh" (Matt. 24:42). In Mark 13:32, our Lord says, "But of that day or that hour knoweth no one, not even the angels in heaven, neither the Son, but the Father." Many are trying by calculations from the data given in Daniel to fix the exact date of our Lord's return, but all such calculations are utterly unreliable. The statements in the book of Daniel were not intended to give us a clue to the exact date of Christ's return, and therefore to attempt to arrive at the date by such calculations is an attempt at the impossible. It is a part of God's purpose and method in dealing with men to keep them in uncertainty on this point. The things which are revealed belong unto us, but this is one of the "secret things (which) belong unto Jehovah our God" (Deut. 29:29). The prophecies of Daniel were extant in the day when Jesus uttered the words found in Matt. 24:36 and Mark 13:32, and doubtless He understood the lessons those prophecies were intended to teach, but He distinctly declares that even He did not know the day nor the hour of His coming again. *As a man* setting an example for us to follow in His steps, He had put away the knowledge of the time of this event. After His resurrection our Lord declared to His disciples that God did not desire us to know the time when He should return again. When His disciples asked Him, "Lord dost thou at this time restore the kingdom of Israel?" He said unto them, "It is not for you to know times or seasons, *which the Father hath set within his own authority*" (Acts 1:6, 7). Let us leave the times where God has put them, *within His own authority.* Any teacher who attempts to fix the date of Christ's return is at once discredited, and it is entirely unnecessary to waste time by wading through his futile calculations.

2. While we are not told the exact time of our Lord's return, we are told that *it will be at such a time as even His disciples think not.* Our Lord says, "Therefore be ye also ready; *for in such an hour as ye think not* the Son of man cometh." It will not be a time when there is a well-nigh universal expectation of our Lord's coming. It will be in a time when men do not expect that coming. Even the faithful and wise servant will be taken unawares, though he will be found doing his Master's will. "Who then," says Jesus, "is the faithful and wise servant, whom his Lord hath set over his household, to give them their food in due season? Blessed is that servant, whom his Lord when he cometh shall find so doing" (Matt. 24:46-47).

3. *The time of our Lord's return will be a time when the world is absorbed in its usual occupations.* "As it came to pass in the days of Noah, even so shall it be also in the days of the Son of man. They ate, they

drank, they married, they were given in marriage, until the day that Noah entered into the ark, and the flood came and destroyed them all. Likewise even as it came to pass in the days of Lot. They ate, they drank, they bought, they sold, they planted, they builded; but in the day that Lot went out from Sodom it rained fire and brimstone from heaven, and destroyed them all; *after the same manner* shall it be in the day that the Son of man is revealed" (Luke 17:26-30). Everything will be going on in its customary way. As already said in another connection, men and women will not be gathered on hilltops in white robes waiting for the descent of their Lord, but men will be engrossed in their ordinary occupations, eating and drinking, marrying and giving in marriage, buying and selling, planting and building; everything shall go on as usual up to the very moment of our Lord's coming. Some would press these words further than this and make them teach that as the days of Noah and Lot were peculiarly wicked days, so will the days of our Lord's return be days of extraordinary wickedness, but this is pressing the words which our Lord speaks here beyond their evident intent. Our Lord meant what He explicitly says, that men will be engaged in their usual occupations, little thinking the Lord is near, and in a moment He will come.

4. *The day of the Lord will not come until after the revelation of the man of sin.* Writing to the Thessalonians who had been disturbed by the thought that the day of the Lord had already come, Paul says, "Be not quickly shaken from your mind, nor yet be troubled, either by spirit, or by word, or by epistle as from us, as that the day of the Lord is just at hand; (English Revision "now present," *i. e.*, "Has actually arrived"). Let no man beguile you in any wise; for it will not be, except the falling away come first, and the man of sin be revealed, the son of perdition, he that opposeth and exalteth himself against all that is called God or that is worshipped; so that he sitteth in the temple of God, setting himself forth as God" (2 Thess. 2:2-4). Of course, the "day of the Lord" is the time of the Lord's coming to the earth. This, as we have already seen, is preceded by His coming into the air to receive the Bride, the Church, unto Himself. There is nothing in Scripture to show that quite an interim may

not intervene between the coming of Christ for His saints in the air and His coming with His saints to the earth. Indeed, there are indications that there must be such an interval. Christ has much to do with His Church before He comes with His Church to deal with the world. Furthermore, we are distinctly taught in the 6th and 7th verses of this same chapter that there is now a restraining power that hinders the manifestation of the man of sin. Paul says, "And now ye know that which restraineth, to the end that he may be revealed in his own season. For the mystery of lawlessness doth already work; *only there is one that restraineth now, until he be taken out of the way.* And then shall be revealed the lawless one, whom the Lord Jesus shall slay with the breath of his mouth, and bring to nought by the manifestation of his coming." It is only natural to presume that this restraining power has something to do with the Church; and the inevitable implication seems to be that the Church must be removed from the earth before "the lawless one" can be revealed on the earth.

5. *The last days and the time of the return of our Lord Jesus will be a time of*

apostasy. We read in I Tim. 4:1, "But the Spirit saith expressly, that *in later times some shall fall away from the faith, giving heed to seducing spirits and doctrines of demons.*" By "doctrines of demons" is evidently meant teachings that evil spirits will promulgate through those men and women who are under their control, such, for example, as the teachings of modern "spiritualism," which might more properly be termed "demonism." The marvelous growth of belief in the "occult" in our day seems to be a fulfillment of this word of prophesy. On every hand men seem to be departing from the faith once delivered to the saints and giving heed to all manner of evil spirits. We are further told by Paul in his second epistle to Timothy that those days shall be "grievous times." He says, "But know this, that in the last days *grievous times* shall come; for men shall be lovers of self, lovers of money, boastful, haughty, railers, disobedient to parents, unthankful, unholy, without natural affection, implacable, slanderers, without self-control, fierce, no lovers of good, traitors, headstrong, puffed up, lovers of pleasure rather than lovers of God; holding a form of godliness, but having denied the power thereof" (II Tim. 5:1-3). These words present to us a remarkably accurate picture of our own time. If one should take up in detail each item in Paul's characterization of the last days, he would find it marvelously fulfilled in our own day. This naturally leads many to suppose that the Lord's coming is very near at hand. However, we should always bear in mind that earnest men of God and students of the Bible have often thought in by-gone days that the coming of the Lord was very near. Luther, for example, thought this centuries ago. These men of the past were not mistaken. The Return of our Lord was very near. Those who were mistaken were those who thought it so far away that they let it have no effect upon their lives. But at the present time, the multiplied iniquities of our day, the apostasy into damning error and unbelief of many professed and hitherto apparently sincere Christians, and of many professedly evangelical preachers, and of numerous professors of theology in seminaries built at great sacrifice by orthodox men and women for the promulgation of truth and not for the breeding of error, the increase of lawlessness on the part of great corporations on the one hand and on the part of the oppressed poor on the other hand, the mutterings preceding the storm of wild anarchy that seems likely soon to break, all these things are signs of His coming which may be very near at hand. Men's hearts are "fainting for fear, and for expectation of the things which are coming on the world" (Luke 21:26). Many of the greatest statesmen of England, America and Germany have forebodings which they scarcely dare to put in words of what lies just a little way ahead of the nations of the earth. But in such days as these our hearts should not faint nor fear. "When these things begin to come to pass" we should "look up and lift up our heads, because our redemption draweth nigh" (Luke 21:28). The darker the day grows, the nearer at hand is the dawn, and just at the moment when things seem unendurable, the brightest, gladdest day the earth ever saw is breaking.

6. *The Return of our Lord is an event, that as far as we know, may occur at any moment.* We are repeatedly exhorted in the Bible to be watching, looking and ready for our Lord's return. In Mark 13:34-36, our

Lord Jesus says to His disciples, "It is as when a man sojourning in another country, having left his house, and given authority to his servants to each one his work, commanded also the porter to watch. Watch, therefore; for ye know not when the Lord of the house cometh, whether at even, or at midnight, or at cock-crowing, or in the morning; lest coming suddenly he find you sleeping." Again in Luke 12:35, 36 our Lord is recorded as saying, "Let your loins be girded about, and your lamps burning; and be ye yourselves like unto men looking for their lord, when he shall return from the marriage feast; that, when he cometh and knocketh, they may straightway open unto him." Still again we read in Matt. 25:13, these words of our Lord, "Watch therefore, for ye know not the day nor the hour." In the preceding chapter, Matt. 24:42, 44, we read, "Watch therefore, for ye know not on what day your lord cometh. Therefore be ye also ready, for in an hour when ye think not the Son of man cometh." If we knew that there were any event, or series of events, that must occur before our Lord comes to receive His own unto Himself, we could not be watching as our Lord in these passages bids us watch. I was once talking with a friend who believed that the tribulation must come before our Lord could come, and I asked him how we could be watching and looking for our Lord if we knew that He could not come for some years yet, namely until after the tribulation had come. He replied, there was "no psychological difficulty at all." But there is a psychological difficulty. It is an absolute impossibility for an intelligent man to be watching for an event that he knows cannot occur for some years. So it is evident from the clear teaching of our Jesus Himself that the coming of our Lord must be an event that, as far as we know, may occur at any moment. There is no event predicted in Scripture, and no series of events, that must occur before our Lord Jesus comes to receive His own unto Himself. It is true there are events that must occur before He comes to the earth with His saints (II Thess. 2), but He may come for us, *as far as we know,* at any moment and it stands us in hand to be always ready, "For in such an hour as ye think not, the Son of man cometh."

But some one will say, "Is not the world to be converted before Jesus Christ comes?"

The simplest answer to this question is to read the Bible descriptions of the state of affairs when our Lord comes again. We read for example in Rev. 1:7, "Behold, he cometh with the clouds; and every eye shall see him, and they that pierced him, and *all the tribes of the earth shall mourn over him.*" This certainly does not picture a converted world, not a world rejoicing at the return of their Lord, but all the tribes of the earth mourning. If possible, even more explicitly we read in Matt. 25:31, 32, "But when the Son of man shall come in his glory, and all the angels with him, then shall he sit on the throne of his glory, and before him shall be gathered all nations; and he *shall separate them one from another,* as the shepherd separateth the sheep from the goats." This certainly does not picture the whole world converted. Still again we read in II Thess. 2:2-4, 8, "To the end that ye be not quickly shaken from your mind, nor yet be troubled, either by spirit, or by word, or by epistle as from us, as that the day of the Lord is just at hand; let no man beguile you in any wise; for it will not be, except the falling away come first, and the man of sin be revealed, the son of perdition, he that opposeth and exalteth himself against all that is called God or that is worshipped; so that he sitteth in the temple of God, setting himself forth as God. . . . And then shall be revealed the lawless one, whom the Lord Jesus shall slay with the breath of His mouth, and bring to nought by the manifestation of his coming." This pictures anything but a converted world at the time of our Lord's return. Our Lord Himself on one occasion said, "Nevertheless, when the Son of man cometh, shall he find faith on the earth?" The clear implication of these words is that when the Lord comes that so far from the whole world being converted, real faith will be a difficult thing to find. Still again in Luke 21:34, 35, "But take heed to yourselves, lest haply your hearts be overcharged with surfeiting, and drunkenness, and cares of this life, and that day come on you suddenly as *a snare; for so shall it come* upon all them that dwell on the face of all the earth." This certainly does not present to us a world already converted at the time of our Lord's Return. In the same way the Holy Spirit, speaking through the Apostle Paul, says in II Tim. 3:1-5, "But know this, that in the last days grievous times shall come. For men shall be lovers of self, lovers of money, boastful, haughty, railers, disobedient to parents, unthankful, unholy, without natural affection, implacable, slanderers, without self-control, fierce, no lovers of good, traitors, headstrong, puffed-up, lovers of pleasure more than lovers of God; holding a form of godliness, but having denied the power thereof; from these also turn away." These verses do not picture a converted world, but a world just as we see it today. There will be two classes, converted and unconverted, at the revelation of Jesus Christ from heaven. The Apostle Paul says, "It is a righteous thing with God to recompense affliction to them that afflict you, and to you that are afflicted rest with us, *at the revelation of the Lord Jesus from heaven* with the angels of his power in flaming fire, *rendering vengeance to them that know not God, and to them that obey not the Gospel of our Lord Jesus;* who shall suffer punishment, even eternal destruction from the face of the Lord and from the glory of his might, *When he shall come* to be glorified *in his saints,* and to be marveled at in all them that believed (because our testimony unto you was believed) in that day" (II Thess.

1:6-10). It is perfectly evident from all these passages that the whole world is not to be converted before the return of our Lord. "But," some one will ask, "how then shall we explain Matt. 24:14, 'And this gospel of the kingdom shall be preached in the whole world for a testimony unto all the nations; and then shall the end come.' Does not this predict a converted world at the coming of the Lord?" It certainly does not. The explanation is found in noticing what is said:

(1.) First of all, this verse tells us that the Gospel is to be preached *"for a testimony,"* to all the nations, not that all the nations will be converted. The Gospel has certainly been preached for a testimony throughout the United States, but no intelligent person would hold that all Americans are converted.

(2.) In the second place, in a sense, and in a Scriptural sense too, the Gospel already has been preached for a testimony to the ends of the world. Paul could say even in his day, "But I say, did they not hear? Yea, verily, their sound went out *into all the earth,* and *their words unto the ends of the world"* (Rom. 18:18). He could further say in Col. 1:23, "The hope of the Gospel which ye heard, which was *preached in all creation under heaven.*"

(3.) In the third place, Matt. 24:44, tells us that the gospel of the kingdom shall be preached in all the world, and "*then* shall *the end* come." The coming of Jesus Christ to receive His own is not the end. It is but the beginning of the end.

But some one will ask, "If the Lord Jesus may come at any moment how can we explain II Thess. 2:14, "Now we beseech you, brethren, touching the coming of our Lord Jesus Christ, and our gathering unto him; to the end that ye be not quickly shaken from your mind, nor yet be troubled, either by spirit, or by word, or by epistle as from us, as that the day of the Lord is just at hand (literally "now present," as in English Revised Version); let no man beguile you in any wise; for it will not be *except the falling away come first,* and the man of sin be revealed, the son of perdition, he that opposeth and exalteth himself against all that is called God or that is worshipped; so that he sitteth in the temple of God, setting himself forth as God." The answer to this is very simple. It is true that the man of sin must be revealed before *"the day of the Lord* is present." But the day of the Lord is not the coming of Christ to receive His church, but that which follows upon it. How closely it may follow it is difficult for us to say. The Thessalonians were troubled by the teaching that had risen among them that the day of the Lord was already at hand, and that they were in the midst of the judgment, "the day of the Lord." They were greatly excited and perturbed by the fact. Paul shows them that this could not be for the "man of sin" who was to be especially dealt with in "the day of the Lord" had not yet been revealed. There is reason to think, as we have already said, that the taking away of the church must precede the revelation of the man of sin. There is a quite widely accepted theory that "the man of sin" has already been revealed in the Pope, or in the Roman Catholic Church: but while the Pope exhibits some of the characteristics of the man of sin he does not fill out the picture. In the Roman Catholic system, as in some other systems of the present day, there is apparently a preparation for "the man of sin," but the man of sin has not yet been revealed.

At this point the question will arise, "Shall

the Church pass through the great tribulation?" In answer to this we would say, that it is clear from the Bible that the Church will pass through "*tribulation.*" Paul and Barnabas taught the disciples in Lystra and Iconium and Antioch "That through many *tribulations* we must enter into the kingdom of God." But to say that the Church will pass through tribulation, or many tribulations, is not at all to say that the Church will pass through "*the great* tribulation." In the great tribulation God deals with a Christ-rejecting world. The tribulation has to do with the Jew primarily and not with the Gentile. The whole book of Revelation after chapter 4:1 has to do with the time after the rapture of the Church. There is much to indicate that the Church will be shielded during this period. Of course, by the Church we mean the true Church, all those who are united to Jesus Christ by a living faith. In connection with the reference to the great tribulation our Lord says, "Watch ye at every season, making supplication, that ye may prevail *to escape all these things* that shall come to pass, and to stand before the Son of man" (Luke 21:36).

There is one other question that will arise

at this point, "Is the world getting better?" To answer this question intelligently we must ask, what is meant by "the world." If you use "the world" in the Biblical sense, it certainly cannot be getting better for we are taught distinctly in I John 5:19, "The whole world lieth in the evil one." In Biblical usage the world is the whole body of men and women outside of those who accept Christ, that is the body of men and women who reject Christ; it lieth "in the wicked one" and certainly in such embrace cannot be gettng better. Furthermore, the Devil is its god. The Apostle Paul says, "*The god of this world* hath blinded the minds of the unbelieving, that the light of the Gospel of the glory of Christ, who is the image of God, should not dawn upon them" (II Cor. 4:4), and, of course, it necessarily is growing worse. But if we mean by "the world"—as men usually do when they ask this question—the entire mass of men, Christians and non-Christians, that go to make up present human society, then it is to be said there are two developments going on side by side at the present time, the development of the kingdom of God and the development of the kingdom of Satan. These two developments will be brought to a crisis when the anti-Christ is developed at the head of the latter and the Christ appears at the head of the former. The crisis will end in a complete victory for Christ and the kingdom of God, as is evident from the foregoing pages of this book. In the meantime, on the one hand God is gathering out of the world a people for His name; as James puts it in Acts 15:14, "God visited the Gentiles, to take out of them a people for his name." The purpose of the preaching of the Gospel of grace in this present dispensation *is not the winning of the whole world for Christ* but *the gathering out of the world a people for His name.* Many people in these days raise the watchcry, "America for Christ," or "The whole wide world for Christ," but those who know their Bibles know that we shall not see "America for Christ" nor "The whole wide world for Christ" in the present dispensation. The Gospel of Grace has not failed—it is accomplishing just what God intended it should accomplish, gathering out of the world a people for His name, the Church, the bride of Christ. These, whom God is gathering out of the world as a people for His name, are growing in the knowledge and likeness of Himself, and the world is of necessity to a certain extent influenced by them. The influence of Christianity is seen in the political, commercial and social life of the day, and in that sense the world might be said to be growing better. On the other hand, every person who is open-eyed to what is going on in the world to-day, must see that there is what the Scripture predicted there would be, the development of the "mystery of lawlessness" (II Thess. 2:7). There is, it is true, at present some restraining power, but nevertheless the "mystery of lawlessness doth already work," resulting in increasing error and apostasy in the *professing church,* as well as out of it, and in the growing immorality (for example along the lines of divorce and impurity and immodesty in dress, etc.) and especially by the development of anarchy or "lawlessness" among all classes of society. In this sense the world is growing worse. We should not be at all disheartened by this fact. It is a fulfillment of prophecy. Indeed, the darkest clouds that are gathering are but harbingers of the golden day that is coming when our Lord Himself shall return and take up the reins of government.

Chapter VI.

OUR ATTITUDE TOWARD THE RETURN OF OUR LORD JESUS.

We should be always ready—We should be looking, expectant—We should be earnestly longing—The preciousness of the words, "Jesus is coming."

"For the grace of God hath appeared bringing salvation to all men, instructing us, to the intent that, denying ungodliness and worldly lusts, we should live soberly, and righteously, and godly in this present world (aion, age) looking for the blessed hope and appearing of the Great God and our Saviour Jesus Christ."

TITUS 2:11-13.

CHAPTER VI.

OUR ATTITUDE TOWARD THE RETURN OF OUR LORD JESUS.

THE all-important practical question for us all in connection with our Lord's Return is what should be our personal attitude toward His coming again. It is this question which is especially answered in the Bible. The Bible treatment of the doctrine is intensely practical.

1. In the first place, WE SHOULD BE READY FOR OUR LORD'S RETURN WHENSOEVER HE MAY COME. We should hearken diligently to our Lord's own commandment "*Be ye also ready,* for in an hour that ye think not the Son of man cometh." We should not only hearken to these words, but we should keep them in mind every day of our life. Every morning when we rise we should say to ourself, "Be ready for your Lord's return, for He may come to-day." Every night before we lie down to sleep we should ask ourselves the

question, "Would I be ready for my Lord's return if He should come before I awake in the morning?" The imminent return of our Lord is the great Bible argument for a pure, unselfish, devoted, unworldly, active life of service. In much of our modern preaching we urge people to live holily and work diligently because death is swiftly coming, but this is never the Bible argument. The Bible argument always is, Christ is coming. Be ready when He comes. This leads inevitably to the question, "What constitutes readiness for the coming of Christ?"

Luke 21:34-36 answers the question, "But take heed to yourselves, lest haply your hearts be *overcharged with surfeiting,* and *drunkenness,* and *cares of this life,* and that day come on you suddenly as a snare, for so shall it come upon all them that dwell on the face of all the earth. But watch ye *at every season, making supplication,* that ye may prevail to escape all these things that shall come to pass, and to stand before the Son of man." To put it in other words, *separation from the world's indulgence of the flesh, from the world's immersion in the affairs of this life* and *intense daily earnestness in prayer* is the first part of preparation for the Lord's return. There are many who do not drink strong drink, who nevertheless live for their bellies (in Paul's homely but impressive way of putting it, "Whose god is their belly.") They eat not for strength for service, but for gratification of appetite, they even eat what they know is harmful. There are others who live very frugally but who are completely sunken in worldly cares; and there are still others who are very active in Christian service but who are neglectful of prayer. They do not *"Watch at every season, making supplication."* None of these are ready for the Master's coming. In the two parables concerning our Lord's Return in Matt. 25:1-30, we see that having oil in our vessels with our lamps, that is, receiving continuous supplies of the Holy Spirit, and fidelity in the use of our talents in our Lord's service, are two all-important factors in readiness for our Lord's return. I would ask every reader of this book, "Have you received the Holy Spirit, and are you constantly receiving fresh supplies of His presence and power?" And I would ask you again, "Are you diligently using for Him all the talents that our Lord Jesus has confided to you?" If you fail at either point, you are not ready for our Lord's return. In I John 2:28, we read, "And now, my little children, abide in him; that, if he shall be manifested, we may have boldness, and not be ashamed before him at his coming." Here we find that abiding in Him now constitutes readiness for Him when He comes. Are you abiding in Him? Have you truly renounced your own wisdom, your own strength, and your own life, and are you daily and hourly just looking to Him for His wisdom and His strength and His life?

2. In the second place, WE SHOULD BE WATCHING AND LOOKING FOR THE COMING OF OUR LORD. Our Lord Himself says, "And be ye yourselves like unto men *looking for their Lord,* when he shall return from the marriage feast; that, when he cometh, and knocketh, they may straightway open unto him. Blessed are those servants, whom the Lord when he cometh shall find *watching*" (Luke 21:36, 37). It is not enough that our lives are right and our service earnest; we should be alert and expectant for the coming of the Lord. A special blessing is here pronounced upon those servants who are watching for the Lord's return. Would that blessing be yours if He should come today? Would He find

you watching? Oh! Let us be watching and expectant and live every hour in the thought of His coming, and never do anything that we would not gladly have Him find us doing if He should come, and never leave anything undone that we would wish that we had done if He should come. Never go any place where you would not be glad to have Him find you if He should come while you were there.

3. But it is not enough to be watching and looking for the Lord's return. WE SHOULD EARNESTLY DESIRE THE COMING OF OUR LORD. In II Pet. 3:12 we read, "Looking for and *earnestly desiring* the coming of the day of God by reason of which the heavens being on fire shall be dissolved, and the elements shall melt with fervent heat." If we love our Lord above all else we will long for His return above all else. How a true wife longs for the return of the husband who is across the sea. No gifts that he can send her during his absence will compensate for the absence of the husband, so the true bride of Christ longs for the return of the heavenly Bridegroom. While she may rejoice in those measures of grace vouchsafed her in the present through the indwelling Christ, she longs for the return of the Bridegroom Him-

self. I once heard one who had been widely proclaimed as a teacher of advanced truth say that there was a time when he was greatly interested in the Second Coming of Christ, but that of late years he had been so taken up with the glory of the indwelling Christ that he had lost interest in the thought of His return. This utterance was thoroughly unscriptural. To me it is incomprehensible on the part of one who really knows the truth about the Return of our Lord. It is well to preach the present privileges of the indwelling Christ, but there is something better than even this, our Lord Himself is coming; we shall see HIM; we shall be caught up to meet HIM; we shall be ever with HIM. And if it is Himself we love and not merely His gifts, no joy and victory that we may know through the indwelling Christ will satisfy the deepest longings of our soul. We shall long for Himself and for that fulness of fellowship with Him that we shall only know when He Himself comes again. There is a crown awaiting those who *"love His appearing."* It is doubtful if there ever was a believer on this earth who knew more experimentally about the glory of the indwelling Christ than the Apostle Paul, yet one of the last things he wrote was, "Henceforth there is laid up for me the crown of righteousness, which the Lord, the righteous judge shall give to me in that day; and not to me only, but also to *all them that have loved his appearing*" (II Tim. 4:8). May I put a plain question to you, Are you longing for Christ's return? If you are not, you may be sure there is something wrong about your life somewhere, or about your relations to your Lord.

Our Lord Jesus is coming again—precious words! How they ought to thrill our hearts! How they do thrill our hearts! How they ought to lead us to inquire diligently lest there be anything in us that will grieve Him at His coming. How they ought to make our hearts burn with the desire to do more and to use our talents more faithfully while He tarries. *THE LORD JESUS IS COMING!* How small these words make the world with its gain and its loss, its pomp and its pride, its pleasure and its pain, its praise and its blame, to appear. OUR LORD JESUS IS COMING! How these words should make us eager to bring our friends to Christ at once lest they be "left" at His coming. OUR LORD JESUS IS COMING! Yes, He is coming, perhaps this year; perhaps this month, perhaps to-morrow; perhaps to-day. Are you ready? Listen once again to His own last and sweetest promise, "Yea, I come quickly."

"AMEN, COME, LORD JESUS."

Collation of Scripture Passages on the Second Coming of Christ for Individual Study

"And beginning from Moses and from all the prophets, He interpreted to them in all the Scriptures the things concerning Himself.'

LUKE 24:27

"And we have the word of prophecy made more sure; whereunto ye do well that ye take heed, as unto a lamp shining in a dark place, until the day dawn, and the day star arise in your hearts" (or "take heed in your hearts until the Day Star arise.")

2 PETER 1:19

COLLATION OF SCRIPTURE PASSAGES ON THE SECOND COMING OF CHRIST FOR INDIVIDUAL STUDY.

I. The Certainty of Christ's Coming Again.

John 14:3; Heb. 9:28; Phil. 3:20, 21; I Thess. 4:16, 17; Acts 3:19, 20; Acts 1:11; John 21:22; Matt. 24:30, 35, 42, 45-51; 25:1-13, 19, 31; Titus 2:13; II Pet. 3:3, 4; Luke 21:34-36; I John 2:28; Rev. 22:20.

II. The Manner of Christ's Coming Again.

1. Personal. Acts 1:11; John 14:3; I Thess. 4:16, 17.
2. Bodily and Visible. Acts 1:11; Heb. 9:28; Matt. 24:30; 24:26, 27; Rev. 1:7.
3. With great publicity. Matt. 24:26, 27; I Thess. 4:16, 17; Rev. 1:7.
4. In the Clouds of Heaven with Power and great Glory. Matt. 24:30 (cf. Ex. 19:9; 34:5; Ps. 97:1, 2; Matt. 17:5; Ps. 104:3; 19:1), Matt. 26:64; Mark 14:62.
5. In the Glory of His Father with the Holy Angels. Matt. 16:27; Mk. 8:38; II Thess. 1:7.
6. In His own Glory. Matt. 25:31.
7. In Flaming Fire. II Thess. 1:8.
8. With a Shout, with the Voice of the Archangel, and the Trump of God. I Thess. 4:16.
9. With all His Saints. I Thess. 3:13.
10. As a thief—unannounced, without warning, unexpectedly, suddenly. Rev. 16:15; I Thess. 5:2, 3; Matt. 24:37-39; 24:44; Luke 17:26-37; II Pet. 3:10; Luke 21:34, 35.

III. The Purposes of Christ's Coming Again.

1. To Receive His Own unto Himself. John 14:3; I Thess. 4:16, 17; John 17:24.

2. To Fashion Anew the Body of our Humiliation. Phil. 3:20, 21.

3. To Reckon with His Servants. Matt. 25:19.

4. To Judge. Ps. 50:3-6; Matt. 13:24-30, 31-43; 25:31-46; John 5:22; II Tim. 4:1, 8; Jude 14, 15; Rev. 20:5-15; Ps. 71:2-4; 96:10-13; 110:2, 3, 6; Is. 2:2-4; Micah 4:1-5; Is. 11:1-5; Mal. 3:1-6; 4:1-3; Matt. 19:28; 3:12; Luke 3:17; Acts 10:42; 17:31; Rom. 2:16; 14:9-12; I Cor. 4:4, 5; II Cor. 5:10; Jas. 5:8, 9.

5. To Bring to Light the Hidden Things of Darkness and to make Manifest the counsels of the heart. I Cor. 4:5.

6. To Render unto Every Man According to his Deeds. Matt. 16:27; II Tim. 4:8; I Pet. 5:4.

7. To Complete the Salvation of His People. Heb. 9:28; I Pet. 1:5.

8. To be Glorified in His Saints. II Thess. 1:10; Col. 3:4.

9. To be United in Marriage with His Betrothed Bride, the Church. Matt. 25:10; Rev. 19:7-9 (cf. Eph. 5:23-32).

10. To Reign as a King. Luke 19:11-15; Matt. 25:31-46; Rev. 19:11-16; 20:4; 11:15; Ps. 2:1-9; Zech. 14:9; Gen. 49:10; Num. 24:16-19; I Sam. 2:7-10; Ps. 18:43-45, 50; 22:27-31; 24:7-10; 45:1-17; 68:31-35; 72:1, 20; 85:1-13; 86:9; 89:3, 4, 19-29, 36, 37; 96:10-13; 102:12-28; 110:1-7; 132:11, 17, 18; Is. 4:1-6; 9:6, 7; 25:1-12; 29:17-24; 33:17-24; 35:1-10; 40:9-11; 42:1-17; 45:6, 20-25; 49:8-26; 52:1-15; 53:12; 54:1-17; 55:313; 56:1-8; 59:15-21; 60:1-22; 61:1-10; 62:1-12; 63:1-6; 65:17-25; 66:10-24; Jer. 3:14-17; 23:1-8; 30:1-11, 18-22; 33:1-26; Ezek. 37:15-28; Dan. 2:31-45; 7:1-28; 8:23-26; Hos. 3:4, 5; Joel

3:1-21; Amos 9:11-15; Ob. 15-21; Micah 4:1-13; 5:2-15; 7:7-20; Zeph. 3:8-20; Hag. 2:20-23; Zech. 3:8-10; 6:12-15; 8:1-13, 20, 23; 9:9, 10, 14-17; 12:1-14; 13:1-9; 14:1-21; Matt. 13:41-43; 19:28-30; 23:37-39; Luke 1:32, 33; 19:27; 22:29, 30; 23:42; Acts 2:30; 3:19-23; I Cor. 15:23-28; Phil. 2:9-11; Heb. 10:13; Rev. 1:5-7; 6:2-17; 17:13, 14.

11. To Deliver Israel in the Day When his Trials and Sufferings shall Culminate. Zech. 14:1-15.

12. To Gather together the Outcasts of Israel. Zech. 8:1-8.

13. To Deliver Israel and Turn Away Ungodliness from Jacob. Rom. 11:25-32; Is. 59:15-21.

14. To Sit as a Refiner and Purifier of Silver. Mal. 3:1-3.

15. To Punish the Inhabitants of the Earth for their Iniquity. Is. 26:20, 21; Jude 14, 15.

16. To Render Vengeance to them that know not God and to them that Obey not the Gospel of our Lord Jesus Christ. II Thess. 1:7-9.

17. To Slay the Lawless One with the Breath of His Mouth and to Bring him to Naught. II Thess. 2:8, 9; Rev. 19:19-21.

18. To Establish a Universal Reign of Righteousness and Godliness upon Earth. Is. 11:1-10.

IV. The Results of Christ's Coming Again.

(Note. The results of Christ's coming again run parallel to the purposes of His coming again, but some passages are better classified under the purposes and others under the results).

1. *AS REGARDS GOD.*

The glory of Jehovah shall be revealed and all flesh shall see it together. Is. 40:3-5, 9-11.

2. *AS REGARDS THE CHURCH.*

(1). The dead in Christ shall rise. I Thess. 4:16; II Cor. 5:1-8.

(2). The bodies of believers shall be transformed into the likeness of the body of His glory. Phil. 3:20, 21; Rom. 8:23-25.

(3). Believers shall be caught up together to meet the Lord in the air to be forever with Him. I Thess. 4:17; John 14:3.

(4). Believers shall be made like Him. I John 3:2.

(5). The Church shall be united in marriage to Him. Matt. 25:10; Rev. 19:7-9; cf. Eph. 5:23-32.

(6). Believers shall be manifested in glory together with Him. Col. 3:4.

(7). Those who love His appearing shall receive the crown of righteousness. II Tim. 4:8.

(8). Faithful shepherds of the flock shall receive a crown of glory that fadeth not away. I Pet. 5:1-4.

(9). His people shall live and reign with Him. Rev. 20:4-6; 5:9, 10; Matt. 19:28; Luke 22:30; Dan. 7:27; II Tim. 2:12; Rom. 8:17; Rev. 22:5.

3. *AS REGARDS ISRAEL.*

(1). They shall mourn over their sin in their former crucifixion of their Messiah. Zech. 12:10-14.

(2). A fountain shall be opened for their sin and their uncleanness. Zech. 13:1, 2.

(3). There shall be great joy among them. Is. 25:8-10.

(4). Israel shall be gathered together from among the nations, from the four corners of the earth, and brought into their own land. Is. 11:11, 12; 27:13; 30:18-26; 32:15-20; 33:13-24; 35:1-9; 37:31, 32; 40:1-11; 49:8-26; 51:9-23; 52:1-12; 60:1-22; 61:4-11; Jer. 3:14-18; 12:14, 15; 23:3-8; 24:4-7; 30:3-22; 32:36-44; 33:1-25;

Ezek. 16:60-63; 20:40-44; 36:8-15, 22-38; 37:11-14, 21-23; Joel 3:1-21; Amos 9:9-15; Ob. 17-21; Micah 5:2-9; Zeph. 1:14-2:7; 3:14-20; Zech. 1:14-21; 8:7, 8; 10:3-12; 12:1-9; 14:1-15; Mal. 3:4-6.

(5). Divided Israel—Ephraim and Judah—shall be united into one nation under one King. Ezek. 37:19-22, 24-28.

(6). Judah shall be saved and Israel shall dwell safely. Jer. 23:5, 6; Rom. 11:26.

(7). Israel shall be cleansed from all their filthiness, and from all their idols, a new heart will be given them and a new spirit put within them; the stony heart shall be taken away from them and they shall be given a heart of flesh. God will put His Spirit within them and cause them to walk in His statutes and they shall keep His judgments and do them. Ezek. 37:23-28; 36:25-31; Jer. 31:31-34.

(8). Israel shall be wondrously multiplied and the waste and desolate and ruined cities shall be rebuilt and the desolate land made like the Garden of Eden. Jerusalem shall be called the City of Truth and shall be filled with peace, prosperity and happiness. Ezek. 36:37, 38; Jer. 31:27, 28; Ezek. 36:33-37; Zech. 8:1-5; Is. 1:24-27; 4:2-6; 25:6-9; 26:1-21; 29:17-24; 44:1-8; 66:5-24.

(9). Israel shall be greatly exalted above the nations. Zech. 8:20-23; 2:8-13; Is. 49:22. 23; 2:1-4; 66:20.

(10). Israel shall go forth to the nations as preachers of the glory of Jehovah. Is. 66:18, 19.

4. *AS REGARDS THE NATIONS AND UNREGENERATE INDIVIDUALS.*

(1). All the tribes of the earth shall mourn over Him. Matt. 24:30; Rev. 1:7.

(2). The kings of the earth and the great of the nations shall hide themselves and call to the mountains and to the rocks to fall on them and hide them from the face of Him who sitteth on the throne and from the wrath of the Lamb. Rev. 6:15-17.

(3). The nations then living upon the earth shall be gathered together before Him for judgment. Matt. 25:31-46.

(At the end of the Millenial reign those who had no part in the first resurrection shall be raised and shall be judged at the judgment of the Great White Throne. Rev. 20:11-15).

(4). The residue of men and all the nations upon whom Jehovah's name is called will seek after the Lord. People shall come and the inhabitants of many cities, many peoples and strong nations, to seek the Lord of Hosts in Jerusalem. Acts 15:16, 17; Zech. 8:20-23; Is. 2:2, 3.

(5). The Lord Christ shall shatter all those who are rebellious against Him. Ps. 2:7-12.

(6). Those who know not God and those who obey not the Gospel of our Lord Jesus Christ shall suffer punishment, even eternal destruction, from the face of the Lord and from the glory of His power. II Thess. 1:7-9.

(7). Every one that is left of the nations and kings and princes shall worship and serve Jesus Christ. Zech. 14:16; Is. 49:7; Rev. 15:4; Ps. 2:8; 72:8-11.

(8). The kingdom of this world shall become the kingdom of our Lord and of His Christ. Zech. 9:10; Rev. 11:15.

(9). War shall cease—peace and plenty shall reign and the righteous shall flourish. Is. 2:4; Micah 4:3, 4; Ps. 72:7, 16.

5. *AS REGARDS HUMAN SOCIETY AS A WHOLE.*

(1). The earth shall be full of the knowledge of the Lord as the waters cover the sea. Is. 11:9.

6. *AS REGARDS THE ANTI-CHRIST AND THE DEVIL.*

(1). The anti-christ shall be put out of the way by the breath of His mouth, and brought to naught by the manifestation of His coming. II Thess. 2:8-9; Rev. 19:19, 20.

(2). The Devil shall be chained and cast into the abyss for a thousand years. Rev. 20:1-3.

(3). Ultimately the Devil shall be cast into the lake of fire where he shall be tormented day and night forever and ever. Rev. 20:7-10.

7. *AS REGARDS THE PHYSICAL UNIVERSE.*

(1). The creation itself shall be delivered from the corruption to which it is now subject into the liberty of the glory of the children of God. Rom. 8:19-21.

(2). Thorns, briars and carnage shall be no more; the wilderness and solitary place shall be glad, and the desert shall rejoice and blossom as the rose. Is. 55:12, 13; 65:25; 32:15; 35:1-10.

(3). There shall be a new heaven and a new earth. II Pet. 3:12, 13; Rev. 21:1.

V. The Time of Christ's Coming Again.

(1). The exact time no man does know nor can know. Matt. 24:36, 42; Mark 13:32; Acts 1:6, 7.

(2). It will be at such a time as even His disciples think not. Matt. 24:44-46.

(3). It will be a time when the world is absorbed in its usual occupations. Matt. 24:37-42; Luke 17:26-30.

(4). Immediately after the tribulation. matters will develop so rapidly that the generation then living shall not pass away until "all these things be accomplished." Matt. 24:29-35.

(5). The Lord Jesus will not **come to the earth with His saints** until after the revelation of the man of sin. II Thess. 2:2-4.

(6). The last days will be a time of apostasy, grievous times, and faith will be hard to find. I Tim. 4:1-3; II Tim. 3:1-5; Luke 18:8.

(7). As far as we know, the Lord may come **for His people in the air** at any moment, for we are repeatedly exhorted to be watching, looking and ready for His return. Mark 13:34, 35, 36; Luke 12:35, 36; Matt. 25:13; 24:42, 44.

(8). It will be a time when there will be both converted and unconverted people upon the earth. Matt. 25:31, 32; Rev. 1:7; II Thess. 1:7-10; 2:2-4, 8; Luke 21:35; II Tim. 3:1-5.

(9). The final end (for which the coming of the Lord is a preparation) will not come until the Gospel of the kingdom shall be preached in all the world for a witness unto all the nations. Matt. 24:14.

VI. The True Attitude Toward Christ's Coming Again.

(1). We should be ready for His coming. Matt. 24:44; Luke 21:34-36; Matt. 25:1-30; I John 2:28.

(2). We should be looking and watching for the coming of our Lord. Luke 12:36, 37; Heb. 9:28.

(3). We should earnestly desire the coming of our Lord. II Pet. 3:12, 13; II Tim. 4:8.

(4). We should pray for our Lord's coming. Rev. 22:20.

(5). We should preach the Second Coming of Christ. I Thess. 4:18.